CW00409547

THE DICTIONARY OF
dangerous
WORDS

Compiled by
DIGBY ANDERSON

Published by the Social Affairs Unit

British Library Cataloguing in Publication Data
A catalogue record of this book is available
from the British Library

THE SOCIAL AFFAIRS UNIT GRATEFULLY
ACKNOWLEDGES THE SUPPORT
OF THE CHARLOTTE AND WALTER KOHLER
CHARITABLE TRUST
FOR THE WORK WHICH MADE
THIS PUBLICATION POSSIBLE

Social Affairs Unit publications represent
the views of their individual authors, not those
of the Unit, its Trustees, Advisers or Director

Book production and typesetting by
Crowley Esmonde Limited
Printed and bound in the United Kingdom

SOCIAL AFFAIRS UNIT
314-322 Regent Street
London W1B 3BB
www.socialaffairsunit.org.uk

ISBN 0 907631 93 2

ACCESS

Way in, or means of approaching a building or information, according to the Oxford English Dictionary (OED). Presumably, at one time it was perfectly in order to say that there was no *access* to, for example, a building or event or institution, without this necessarily being taken to be a bad thing. But now *access* is not a neutral term. It is used only in special, politically correct contexts. Where there is *access* all barriers are down for the sake of a theoretical equality (qv), irrespective of whether there might be reasons for denying *access* in certain cases.

In education *access* is used to signify that the school or university (qv) in question has dropped all its entry standards, in an effort to appear welcoming and non-elitist. In the arts the term is used to pretend that great works are not sometimes difficult. In both cases, *access* projects are patronising and misleading, for they deprive people of the rewards they might have been able to get had they actually confronted an artistic challenge or passed an entrance exam.

Access is also given as the justification for redesigning tens of thousands of ancient buildings so as to enable people in wheelchairs to get in. This provides a fertile hunting ground for activists, but as the late Quentin Crewe, himself disabled and in a wheelchair, bravely pointed out, it is by no means clear that it is necessary for one's quality (qv) of life that one be able to visit every historic (qv) site oneself whether one is disabled or not.

ANTHONY O'HEAR

ACCIDENT

According to the Concise Oxford Dictionary: event without apparent cause (qv), unintentional act, chance, fortune. In its traditional sense the word was applied to events such as train crashes, boat capsizings, falling over and grazing a knee, or a sudden attack of sickness and diarrhoea. It is still applied to these events and it retains the sense of the unexpected. The word 'victim' (qv) is also still used of those to whom *accidents* happen. But modern society is averse to the idea that things can happen by chance; it resents the suggestion that there are events beyond its control. It is even more averse to the idea that unpleasant things can happen without anyone being to blame. So, after any *accident* the first demand is for an inquiry, better still a 'full and wide ranging inquiry' to find out the cause. The ultimate object of such an inquiry is find someone to blame for the *accident*.

Energetic blame-hounds are not content to find individuals such as train drivers to blame for train crashes. They prefer more remote causes and bigger causes to do with the 'structure' of society. An *accident* may be blamed on the privatised train company, or better still, the privatisation of the railways in general, or just privatisation per se or even the pursuit of profit. Other favourite objects for denunciation are lack of resources (qv) and the persons or policies responsible for inadequate resources being put into safety. The grazed knee is the fault of the landowner who did not put up a notice warning that shingle is slippery or that of the local authority which did not provide the resources necessary for a free bus service to school and thus obliged the boy to walk down the shingle path. The diarrhoea is caused by sloppy hygiene in the profit-seeking food industry or lack of health inspections caused by cutbacks in local government staffing caused by lack of resources. An eminent politician once blamed an *accident* on the absence of a culture of safety.

Implicit in all this is the idea that risks can be reduced to zero and that this would be a good thing whatever the cost. This is encapsulated in the pompous and pig-headed recitation of the word 'unacceptable' to describe recalcitrant

realities. *Accidents* do not happen by *accident* any more.
DIGBY ANDERSON

A DULT

An *adult* was a grown-up or mature person. There was always a certain amount of untidiness about the meaning. Systematically-minded people used to complain that young people could fight for their country and marry (age 16) and go to prison (age 17) long before they could vote (age 21). If they were mature enough for one, why not for the other. The same disputes continue. The British Government recently introduced regulations to stop young people letting off their own fireworks before the age of 18 while allowing the same young people to be seduced by homosexuals at 16. What is new in the banger-bugger and other current disputes is that the rival camps now artfully deploy the age terms to fit their cause (qv). So when left-wing (qv) persons want young people to receive housing benefits (qv) so that they can live away from their parents or/and engage in homosexual acts, they refer to them as *adults* or 'young *adults*'. When they want to protect them from the sellers of cigarettes, fizzy drinks and bangers, they call them children or 'vulnerable young people'. Their opponents do the same, in reverse. The fact that both can get away with this shows a society which no longer knows what an *adult* is.
DIGBY ANDERSON

A FFIRM

Once it meant to state or declare something strongly. Now it is one of a huge list of psychological and social (qv) needs (qv) that modern (qv) persons are alleged to have, everyone needs to have himself affirmed. And once persons have these needs they are also endowed with a 'right' to have them satisfied. Thus children who perform badly at school need not to be told that they have performed badly (the truth), still less be punished. They need to be *affirmed* and, possibly, have their incorrect answers *affirmed* too. In the social system there are queues of people from single parents to promiscuous (qv) homosexuals whose main need is that their cultures be *affirmed*, even 'celebrated' and indulged with taxpayers' largesse.

If they are found not to be *affirmed*, celebrated and subsidized, then that will be because someone is denying them their rights (qv). The new use of *affirm* can thus produce a whole industry dedicated to finding denied sub-cultures, identifying those doing the denying and seeking reparations.

DIGBY ANDERSON

ALTERNATIVE

Now used to give legitimacy to behaviour or 'orientation' once seen as bizarre, unusual or even wrong. *Alternative* cultures may involve rejection of the material world, of the Western economic and political system, of the world of work, of a fixed residential address, of conventional forms of healing and medicine, and of institutional religion. The archetypal beings of *alternative* society in the post-war period are the hippie and the new-age traveller; earlier examples include John the Baptist.

Traditionally *alternative* signifies one option relative to another, but in modern times it is used to describe a form which aspires, however covertly, to supplant another: an *alternative* is now a pretender. In this sense *alternative* has been much used since the late 1960s and was borrowed by the Church of England in 1980 as the title of its collection of devalued forms of worship and sundry ephemera, The Alternative Service Book. While quietly conceding that the traditional Book of Common Prayer of 1662 remained the standard of worship and doctrine, bishops and others bore down upon the clergy to establish the *alternative* as the norm until, in due time, the faithful grew to be unfamiliar with their own standard.

Alternatives, then, may be of different types. The *alternative* society of hippies, vegans, neo-pagans, western Buddhists and homeopathic medicine is generated by its members; it is of the organic (qv) type. The Alternative Service Book of the Anglican church was commissioned by its governing body and propagated in a pastoral letter by its archbishops; its initiation is of the hierarchical type. In both, however, the term *alternative* signifies an intention, more explicit in the first and more concealed in the second, to dislocate existing forms and destabilize existing standards.

ROGER HOMAN

A MAZING

Largely a journalistic foible. Time after time I am told that someone has made an *amazing* attack, an *amazing* statement or released *amazing* figures. Not so. They have actually made an attack, a statement, or released some statistics. If I am going to be amazed, then I shall decide it. I don't need the reporter to tell me to be amazed.

FREDERICK FORSYTH

A PPROPRIATE

This is both a useful and even a nice word, though it has one tough meaning which sends a chill. To *appropriate* funds, for instance, is to sequester or grab them, as a bailiff or a court or a socialist regime might do. More generally, to be *appropriate* is to be fitting, proper, fit for purpose, apposite. All sorts of things can be judged to be or not be *appropriate*. But it does not best fit, say, the rightness of a spanner or coat for the job in hand.

The word is at its best when we use it of human behaviour. Thus it is, of course, proper (*appropriate*, even) that a judge will use the word when pronouncing sentence, and say that only a life sentence (or only probation) would be *appropriate* to a particular crime. In this use both the aptness of a judgement (does it fit the crime?) and proportionality (does its severity match the crime's seriousness?) also point to how useful the word can be when also applied to regulations.

However, *appropriate* is one of those words which has fallen into disrepute, like 'reasonable' and 'acceptable'. Put on a strangulated lace-curtained accent of surburban lower-middle-class refinement and discuss the 'reasonableness' of the day's weather ('it is reasonably warm', etc) and you get some of the drift of this. Now refine the voice to include the downwardly mobile tones of a campaign harridan and discuss whether such behaviour is 'acceptable': in this use, very little behaviour is. Now take the same sort of voice discussing whether a judge's being male, middle class and middle aged is *appropriate*, or whether it is *appropriate* to describe a lesbian as a diesel (and whether it is more or less *appropriate* to do so in male or in lesbian company) and you get to see the pickle into which *appropriate* has fallen. Take, for instance, the Commission for Racial Equality's use of it when it says, 'reference to the fact that an individual is a Traveller, Gypsy or Irish Traveller should only be made when it is relevant and *appropriate*'. In other words, only when you are about to say something nice about the qualities which attach to people by virtue of this bit of ethnicity, which is otherwise to be denied. The context of this usage is right if it speaks of propriety, fittingness, suitability but the implied censorship (qv), the political correctness, the bossiness, are not. In short, *appropriate* has been appropriated by all the wrong people.

RICHARD D NORTH

A SPIRATION

The word lies somewhere above a vague hope but below an actual government policy commitment. When the British Prime Minister wants to downgrade a manifesto promise which he is unable to deliver, it is renamed an *aspiration*. It is also regularly used to describe the ambition of a social class or grouping, with the subtext that it is immoral to deny something so designated. Often used at party conferences, if ordinary working people and their families are held to have an *aspiration* for something, then, whether or not it is in the overall national interest (qv) to give it to them, they must automatically get it. You can never simply deny someone's *aspiration*, however greedy, selfish or short-sighted it might be.

ANDREW ROBERTS

B ACKWARD as in BACKWARD CHILD

Obsolete because banned. People who do not learn as quickly as others and people with physical disabilities have both been subjected to stigma. Decent people always regarded such stigma as cruel and wrong. But now those once stigmatised have been conscripted into the ranks of a minority with special rights (qv). Chief among these is the right to be renamed. The quaint supposition is that the old names are bound up with the stigma so if we can only stop calling cripples cripples and call them handicapped (qv) or disabled or differently-abled the stigma will be reduced. Thus the term for *backward* children is continually being ousted in a series of revolutions including children-with-learning-difficulties, late developers and children with special needs (qv). But as is obvious from another totally different case, the change from negro to black (qv) to Afro-Caribbean has done, unfortunately, nothing to remove the stigma so unfairly attached to these people. Indeed those who enjoy stigmatising such groups usually take up the new word, give it a sarcastic intonation, accompany it with a collusive mocking expression and apply it with relish.

Playing with words in cases of stigma has a rather dubious history. Robert Procter's The Nazi War on Cancer points out that in Germany the change of the words cripple to handicapped and idiot and asylum to retarded and clinic were orchestrated by physicians and bureaucrats organizing the murder of the physically and mentally handicapped.

DIGBY ANDERSON

B ACKWARD as in BACKWARD COUNTRY

A strictly non-PC term to describe most countries of Africa – without actually naming them.

Backward countries were later reclassified hopefully as 'developing countries' in order to justify pouring in countless billions of pounds in the name of 'foreign aid'.

When, decades later, 'developing countries' stubbornly exhibited few signs of developing, they were re-reclassified – delicately but more truthfully – under the anodyne title of 'less developed countries', grandly rendered in official texts as 'LDCs'.

The death in 1999 of Julius Nyerere prompted the Daily Telegraph to print an extensive obituary, less of the noble but misguided founder of 'African socialism' than of the economic and political shambles to which he had reduced Tanzania.

RALPH HARRIS

B ENEFIT

Once meant an advantage, something people might want. Now, often preceded by 'unemployment (qv) /disability/housing'. In the course of the twentieth century the state has provided a welfare (qv) 'safety net'. This idea has been widely endorsed by free market writers, for

example Friedrich Hayek, wishing presumably to make the free market more palatable to those fearing redundancy or low pay. However, as Anthony de Jasay has pointed out, the concept is a Trojan Horse that has spilled out an invading army of distorting taxes and subsidies into the market economy. The unemployed (especially those who can command only low-paid jobs) receive effectively permanent support for failing to get work; to induce them ('please') to take work, low-paid workers are offered further means-tested *benefits* (the now-renamed 'working families tax credit' plus housing *benefit*) once back in a job. But the effect is little incentive to take the job and, if taken, little incentive to improve the job for fear of losing *benefits*. To persuade some of those long-term unemployed to come off the widely-known register, the state is also generous with 'disability *benefit*'. All these *benefits* wind up inducing their recipients either to stay unemployed or to stay in a second-rate job. This creates dependency which is ultimately damaging to them. It also costs the taxpayer a lot of money. *Benefits* did you call them?
PATRICK MINFORD

B LACK
An ambiguous social category used by policy advisers, race-relations agitators and 'critical (qv) sociologists'. Its boundaries are infinitely malleable depending on what particular tendentious argument about the over- or under-representation of *blacks* in education, senior positions, particular professions, crime statistics, prison, sport, vegetarianism or freemasonry is being advanced. Sometimes it means Afro-Caribbeans (who used to be called West Indian negroes) but it can, if necessary, be extended to include all manner of people who neither see themselves as *black* nor are perceived as such by others for the simple reason that they are not *black*. British Kashmiris, Punjabis, Gujaratis and Bengalis often get

categorized as black as indeed do Palestinians and Cypriots. The Irish should watch this space.
CHRISTIE DAVIES

B OURGEOIS

Noun and adjective from the French term for a city-dweller. The 'bourgeoisie' in France composed the Third Estate under the ancien regime, and *bourgeois* denoted one category of membership in cities such as Geneva in the eighteenth century. In the nineteenth century, especially in France, the term *bourgeois* expressed the contempt some members of this middle class felt for the way of life in which they had been reared. *Bourgeois* stood for everything that was comfortable, philistine, narrow and commercial. The 'bourgeoisie' were endlessly abused by Bohemians from one vantage point, and socialists from another. Baudelaire thought the business of art was to shock them, while D H Lawrence, picking up a French affectation, declared 'how beastly the *bourgeois* is, especially the male of the species'. In Marxist thought, the 'bourgeoisie' was the ruling class of capitalism (qv) and it had to be overthrown, a truth little affected by the fact that most of the revolutionaries, like most of the Bohemians, were themselves *bourgeois*. The term thus stands for a civil war within the educated classes of the Western world and a by now rather stale affectation of aristocratic contempt for commerce.
KENNETH MINOGUE

C ANON

From Greek kanon, measure. 1. In classical Roman education, a shortlist of authors and texts selected to serve as standards of achievement in their respective genres. 2. In the Christian tradition, the body of texts judged by the Church (qv) to deserve inclusion in the Scriptures; acknowledged as authoritative. 3. In contemporary academia, an abbreviated version of 'western *canon*', a mythical entity in the folklore of radical humanism. An unspecified body of texts judged by an unspecified authority to deserve inclusion in a curriculum of education, so as to exclude texts subversive to dominant cultural norms.

This usage results from the illicit substitution of *canon* (2), appropriate (qv) to ecclesiastical settings, for *canon* (1), appropriate and necessary to an educational setting which requires judgement about what is worth the investment of a student's limited time and energies. Such obfuscation permits professors to teach ephemeral, politically programmatic and superficially thrilling authors that would not stand the test required by invocation of *canon* (1). This myth was originally invented by professors nostalgic for the era of campus protest who, having become the establishment, needed a repressive meta-establishment to stand against in defiance (nb: dead white males command no tear-gas). In time, however, the myth of the 'western *canon*' found its way into the counter-countercultural folklore of young conservatives, for whom anything attacked by leftists must be good.

MARK SHIFFMAN

CAPITALISM

Abstract noun denoting the commercial aspects of the modern world treated as a system determining culture, law, society and (in Marxist thought) all other aspects of Western life. *Capitalist* originated as a term of abuse in the French Revolution, and soon acquired its Homeric epithet 'bloated'. *Capitalism* emerged in the middle of the nineteenth century as the most general expression of the socialist hatred of the modern world. Socialists picked out as *capitalist* the most inhumane and mechanical aspects of European life. Marx thought that capital itself had magical properties. It could, for example, turn a wrinkled old man into a suitable mate for a beautiful young thing, and the way in which it swirled around the world caused peasants to move to cities, and migrants to populate the new world. It was a horrible but impressive monster, and the business of socialists was to transform it by changing the basis of social and economic life away from profit towards need.

By the end of the nineteenth century, however, the term had lost some of its pejorative tone and was being used by thinkers such as Max Weber, and later Joseph Schumpeter as denoting the modern world from an economic point of view. Some economists, perhaps most notably Friedrich Hayek, began defending *capitalism*, something that from a socialist point of view was akin to devil worship.

During the twentieth century its enemies were indefatigable in attempting to overthrow *capitalism*, but that endeavour came to an end with the collapse of Soviet Communism. Since that time, the project has been to transform the economy (something thought to be cold, brutal and selfish) into a community (qv) by using the authority of a democratic state. Socialists often anticipate the fruition of their ambitions by plaintively using the term 'late' (qv) *capitalism* but although the modern world is certainly changing its character, there is no sign that its capitalist aspects are disappearing.

KENNETH MINOGUE

CAUSE

1. An objective or end that is perceived (usually by the left-wing intelligentsia) to be worthy, especially of compulsory support via taxation and regulation, as in 'Your taxes will be used for a good *cause*', 'Curtailing individual liberty is justified by this good *cause*'. In this usage, cause actually refers to an effect. Prime examples include social (qv) welfare (qv), environmental purity, stakeholder interests, etc.

Ironically, this usage is most common

amongst those who deny strict causality (see 2 below). It is, however, unclear how, if *causes* do not necessarily produce their effects, the property confiscated can be expected to achieve the supposedly worthy ends specified.

2. That which precedes and necessarily brings about an effect: when the causal conditions (eg combustible material, sufficient heat, oxygen) are assembled, the effect (fire) necessarily follows: everywhere, every time.

Since the writings of David Hume, and especially the Enquiry Concerning Human Understanding (1748) became popular, however, this notion of strict causality has (wrongly) come to be in doubt. Causation is now often considered to be unreliable, because the Humean doctrine is believed to eliminate the 'real world' mechanism that makes causation work.

Originally afflicting only credulous philosophers, suspicion concerning strict causality has increasingly been adopted by the intelligentsia, who seem to believe that the absence of causality will relieve them (and their favoured charges) of responsibility. Their argument is presumably that if nothing necessarily leads to anything else, and anything might follow from anything, no one can be held personally responsible for what happens or fails to happen. There is, therefore, no reason why anyone should bother to bring about the conditions of good results.

ELAINE STERNBERG

C ENSORSHIP

Formerly used to refer to the state banning a book, film, play or painting, or prohibiting certain news from being published. It has acquired two novel meanings. The first is that something is 'censored' if the state has obstinately refused to provide taxpayers' money to promote it. A play by the former Trotskyist Tariq Ali which attacked British Prime Minister Tony Blair, was said to be 'censored' because the state-subsidized Royal National Theatre would not produce it. The fact that it was put on in another theatre, and received less than enthusiastic reviews, did nothing to reduce this charge. The second is when a newspaper or magazine does not provide regular prominent column space for views antithetical to its own or which excoriate its proprietor. The fact that the (London) Times does not carry daily attacks on Rupert Murdoch is cited as a particularly abhorrent example of 'censorship', even though other newspapers more than make up for the omission. Some would take this second category even further. McDonalds (qv) is 'censoring' its opponents by not providing, at its own expense – that is, its consumers' expense – leaflets attacking the hamburgers they so much enjoy.

MICHAEL MOSBACHER

CHILD ABUSE

What might seem to suggest no more than rudeness to a child or children – insulting them or telling them off – moved in one jump to mean their sexual violation. Whether as a result of residual sentimentality about children or the sexual confusion of the times, child sexual abuse has been identified as the most odious and wickedest crime it is possible to commit – the only one which will find no defenders anywhere.

By one remove, *child abuse* has since been applied to any violence against a child, including physical chastisement. It is only a small step before it is seen in any attempt to rebuke or discipline a child. Such activity will then carry at any rate some of the odium attaching to sexual violation, and nobody will dare contradict a child or say it is wrong.

AUBERON WAUGH

CHILD CARE

Once something natural parents did. Now a tax-funded state scheme under which abused children are removed from their natural parents to be 'cared for' by the government in a variety of ways from individual foster homes to larger institutions. To avoid such children bonding with a substitute parent they are regularly bounced around the system. Carers included, until very recently, known convicted child molestors, and half of all girls in care are impregnated prior to turning 16. Currently under investigation by the Audit Commission, the system costs over £2 billion and cares for 50,000 plus children in a given year.

Alumni of the system are on the streets homeless, on drugs, on benefit (qv), or in jail. Whereas one often comes across adoptees who turn out to be successful, the author has failed to find a successful alumnus of the state *child-care* system.

JOHN BLUNDELL

CHURCH

Once a building in which Christians worshipped God. The introit for the common of the dedication of a *church* read, 'How dreadful is this place; this is the house of God and the gate of heaven'. A *church* was a holy place where men went to find God. Because they were sinful and He was a God of loving judgment, it was indeed both a dreadful place and the gate of heaven. Because it was His house, men made it and the liturgy they used there as beautiful as they could. In *church* men turned towards God, considered His nature, commands and judgment and second coming and faced east in the direction of that coming.

Most contemporary *churches* do not inspire dread or look much like gates to heaven. Often today a *church* is not a place of beauty but of stunning banality, its liturgy trite and ugly. There is little to distinguish the building from a health centre or community hall; which is fitting because increasingly men face and 'celebrate' each other there rather than God's rising sun and resurrection. They do not tremble as they enter these dismal places nor feel themselves on the brink of eternity. The church is simply one more place where they can learn to feel good about themselves and enjoy second rate coffee.

DIGBY ANDERSON

CIVIL as in CIVIL SOCIETY

Usually used in two complementary but distinct senses. First, the term *civil society* is used, across the political spectrum, to describe those voluntary associations which flourish, or ought to flourish, quite apart from the machinery of central government. Appeal is usually made to Tocqueville's classic exposition, in Democracy in America, of intermediary institutions such as churches, associations, guilds, etc. Conservatives, contractarians and communitarians alike voraciously deplore the alleged loss or decline of *civil society*. Secondly, the term connotes a mode of being together, characterized not by partisan or racial bickering or violence (qv), but rather by 'civility', good manners and decency.

Almost invariably, *civil society* is held to be not something that emerges naturally, but something lost which must be restored – the object of some project whose end is categorically unlimited, as with agricultural production or real estate development. In the process, *civil society* becomes not a description of a mode of living together, but an end state to be achieved. So, *civil society* literature speaks of 'growing (sic) *civil society*'. Countless organizations are devoted to 'constructing' or 'building' *civil society*. As a response to alleged rampant individualism and statism (both of which are identified as corrosive of *civil society*), *civil society* is marketed simultaneously as a substantive solution to social ills and as a slogan. Perhaps, in the USA, we can expect a *civil society* cheer at the next Super Bowl half-time show.

The sporting image is not entirely inapt –

the apparent decline in bowling leagues (the famous sociologically-demonstrated phenomenon of 'bowling alone') has been paradigmatically adduced as evidence of a decline in *civil society*. Yet most non-profit organizations devoted to promoting *civil society* seem more interested in signing up party voters than league bowlers. Most pernicious is the co-opting of *civil society* by the state itself. Apparently we do not yet have a Federal programme for league bowling – perhaps league bowling has declined because of Federally-funded midnight basketball leagues – but the state is not about to take a back seat on the *civil society* bandwagon. Countless state-sponsored projects and myriad mandatory activities are poised to ensure we are provided with the *civil society* we 'deserve'. But evidently the *civil society* we want to 'grow' needs the considerable fertilization of our tax dollars. Can the flower of *civil society* grow through the increasing thickness of fertilizer or will the stench choke it off?

It is hard to object to *civil society* (bumper sticker: 'I'm pro *civil society*'), just as one is hard pressed to 'be against' other good things like children, puppies and flowers blooming in the springtime. But one wonders whether energy spent talking about and promoting *civil society* might be better spent not in legislative halls or foundation boardrooms but in churches, guilds and the local bowling alley.

TODD BREYFOGLE

C LEANSING

A form of cleaning. Since the mid 1990s, *cleansing* has come to be used almost exclusively to describe the ridding of whole countries of ethnic (qv) or other groups that incumbent authorities find troublesome, as in 'ethnic *cleansing*'. It is a euphemism for mass eviction and massacre adopted first by its perpetrators, and then by the media. The term is now so widely used that it effectively excludes all honest descriptions of the phenomenon, even by those who deplore it. This euphemistic usage is a perversion of an archaic (Biblical) usage, where *cleansing* was used to refer to purification from sin, or ridding of leprosy.

Until the 1990s, this term's modern usage was mainly in the context of: a. selling special skincare products. Whereas hands and male bodies are simply cleaned of dirt by soap, it was suggested that women's facial pores needed to be more gently cleansed, by cosmetic products (often called '*cleansing* cremes'); b. Yoga, where *cleansing* breaths were supposed to help refocus and redirect attention; a similar usage is sometimes found in natural childbirth, where *cleansing* breaths are supposed to help make labour less painful.

ELAINE STERNBERG

CLIENT

One of the quintessential words of our non-judgemental age. Once it suggested a relationship of equals, freely entered into. On the one hand was an individual seeking services and ready to pay for them, the *client*; on the other was the individual or firm contracting to provide those services. Now the idea has been taken over by institutions who wish to foster the misleading impression that they are involved in an equal partnership with those who are, in fact, obliged to come to them for services, often provided by the state and financed by the taxpayer.

Citizens who receive welfare benefits (qv) are now routinely referred to as *clients*. The unemployed are *clients* of the 'job clubs' that have replaced the old labour exchanges and employment offices (yet other products of the great euphemism machine). Criminals on parole are now *clients* of the probation service; similarly, the wretches who fall into the hands of the council social (qv) services departments.

And some hospitals treating the mentally ill have now taken to calling these patients *clients*.

The idea, clearly, is to remove any suggestion of stigma from the individual who finds himself in any demeaning relationship with authority. The individual is not in any way beholden or obliged, but much esteemed and free to walk away – just like a *client*. Thus we are all equal. And we certainly don't judge.

DERRICK HILL

CLOSET
Formerly a small room for Americans to hang their coats in. Now inhabited by those who can still distinguish between the private and the public (qv) spheres and know what is appropriate to each and do not believe that their whole character is defined by their sexual orientation. Those who denounce homosexuals who are in the *closet* for 'not being true to themselves' confuse sincerity with voyeurism.

MICHAEL MOSBACHER

CODE OF PRACTICE
A pretence, usually in written form, of high ethical and professional standards.

In recent years, *codes of practice* have been widely introduced by professional bodies and business organizations. Ostensibly, they are drawn up as means of regulating behaviour and of ensuring for clients and consumers certain minimum standards of moral conduct or quality of service.

Codes stress procedure rather than responsibilities, and those who observe them easily lose sight of the values they are supposed to enshrine. The Mosaic code included 'thou shalt not kill' as a formula for preserving life: it did not cover the possibility encountered by Bonhoeffer that by killing one villain – Hitler – the lives of millions of others might have been saved. So it is with professional *codes of practice* that the letter is exclusive of the purpose. When children on an outdoor pursuits course are drowned at sea or lost down a pothole, the question asked is whether those in charge were following the relevant *code of practice*. If upon enquiry it is shown that they were doing so, the assurance given is that the code will be revised. The teachers or organizers are charged with no responsibility over and above observance of the code. So codes reduce responsibility from the spirit to the letter. They exonerate those who adhere to them. Lives may be lost but the professionals are saved by their *codes of practice*.

Codes are not to be confused with 'Guidelines' which are equally fashionable. Guidelines are less directive. Professionals may be at fault if they ignore guidelines but they may also be culpable if they follow them. Guidelines may not rescue teachers who could not rescue their pupils.

ROGER HOMAN

COMMUNITY (I)

Formerly referred to the people as a whole and its connotations were friendliness, co-operation and warm-heartedness. It was an altogether more homely phrase than 'society' or 'the public'. But now it has been hijacked by every special interest group going. So we hear of 'the black (qv) *community*', 'the Irish *community*' and 'the homosexual *community*' – presumably the last is a *community* without children. The Independent once referred to 'London's sado-masochistic *community*'.

The new usage is far from benign. It is self-defeating for it does not produce the old usage's homely sense of unity but actually creates the ghetto mentality. As a classic piece of newspeak it exactly reverses the word's original meaning. In the mouths of a hundred special interest groups *community* now in fact means 'sect'.

PETER MULLEN

COMMUNITY (II)

Almost anyone can enjoy being in a *community* – Christians, Muslims, ethnic (qv) groups, urban dwellers, the countryside, pensioners, the young, Europeans. All can be pressure groups on government, demanding popular attention, media coverage, defying opposition to their 'good cause (qv)'. Politicians love *communities* because they harvest the votes.

MARJORIE SELDON

COMPASSION

Denotes both an emotion of fellow-feeling towards others and the acts of generosity that are prompted by such an emotion.

Such acts are proper subjects for the sociology of morals. For distress over the sufferings of others is a universal aspect of human behaviour: the relief of such distress is understandably deemed a moral obligation. Differences are bound to arise over what constitutes distress and as to who the 'others' may be in any particular context – eg the family, the tribe, etc. Animals have also been thought worthy of *compassion* from humans – but not normally from other animals. Sociologists have shown how the range of such obligations has been extended over time.

So far so good – morally and intellectually. A further step is taken in political rhetoric (and in some social analysis aligned with such rhetoric). It can there be argued *a priori* that *compassion* is a source or vehicle of social justice. Such an argument looks beyond the compassionate acts of *individuals* (which can be stigmatised as charity) and moves swiftly to justify institutionalised *collective* action – generally by officials of the State designed to redistribute resources from the better-off to the worse-off members of a society. *Compassion* is thus depersonalized into the arrangements of the welfare state and is manifested through the payment of taxes – so that what to some appears the acceptance of a

tax-burden is turned into the practice of socially applauded virtue. This rhetoric may be subject to diminishing returns. But it enables politicians to appear to promote virtue through the State's power to tax and absolves the (often worthy) objects of *compassion* from the indignity of showing direct personal gratitude to their bene-factors.
JULIUS GOULD

CONSENSUS
Implies disagreement, so results in compro-mise. This does not matter overmuch when truth is not at stake. It matters a great deal when real-ity is compromised. If those who hold the view that two and two make four meet with those who hold that two and two make six and arrive at a *consensus* that two and two make five, *consensus* has become nonsense.

The medical establishment, particularly in the USA, is given to summoning groups of 'experts' to provide a *consensus* statement about matters of current controversy such as diet. Unfortunately the resulting interpretations, although seriously flawed, are given great weight. They are flawed because the chosen 'experts' are of a like mind and truly dissident voices are not included in the *consensus* panel. As a result, many people have been harmed by *consensus* views on, for example, the level of blood pressure at which people should take pills. *Consensus* is dangerous because it ignores and undervalues the dissident.
JAMES McCORMICK

CONSENT
Compulsion (as in 'age of *consent*').
DAVID WOMERSLEY

CONSULTATION
The practice of disarming opposition by involving innocent third parties in a policy of

mischievous tendency upon which you are already resolved; as in, 'the castration and spaying of heterosexuals will be implemented only after the widest possible *consultation*'.
DAVID WOMERSLEY

CONSUMERIST

Older dictionaries have no mention of *consumerists*. They know about consumers, who are users of articles as opposed to producers who produce them. *Consumerists*, though, are happy to remedy the dictionaries' omission. They point out that consumers have interests (qv). These interests, allegedly, need defending, because the consumers are many, innocent and out of contact with each other, whereas the producers are well-organized and out to fleece the consumers. Generously the *consumerists* offer to represent the consumers.

What the *consumerists* do not mention is that the many divided consumers also have many and divided interests. One might want his beer to be strong, another cheap, another linked to a fashionable football star, another in a recyclable bottle, another with a label with lots of information about health risks and 'units', another with a label showing a lady with no clothes on. These interests not only diverge, they compete and some are in opposition to others. In one sense consumers are opposed to each other much more than producers. If producers can find out the dominant wants of consumers, they can make money out of pleasing them and there is harmony of interest with the majority of consumers. Whereas consumers pushing for cheap food, for instance, have definitely been in opposition to those wanting organic (qv), healthy (qv) and fashionable food. To take another example, the true enemy of those consumers who want to keep their High Street shops are the other consumers who switch allegiance to out-of-town centres.

There is then no such thing as the consumers' interest – in the singular. Thus there is no one thing for *consumerists* to represent. The claim to represent the interest of consumers is fraudulent. Further, with some exceptions, *consumerists* do not have systematic procedures for consumers to vote on their preferences. Again, the producers do: every day their sales tell them what people will buy and at what price. The reality (qv) may be, then, that producers, whom many *consumerists* characterize as opposed to consumers, represent the majority of those consumers far more accurately and effectively than do the self-appointed *consumerists*. Perhaps it is as well that many dictionaries deny consumerists a mention.

DIGBY ANDERSON

COUNSELLING

The original word meant the giving of wise advice. The King James' Bible tells us, 'And King Rehoboam took counsel with the old men, that had stood before Solomon his father while he yet lived, saying, What counsel give ye me to return answer to this people?'

King Rehoboam would be astounded if he met a modern counsellor. She would seem more like a puppet than a human being. If the king cupped his chin the counsellor would follow suit; if he wept the counsellor's eyes would brim; if he looked stern his companion's face would instantly set in formal lines. Every time the king spoke, he would hear the last three words of his sentence come out of the counsellor's mouth.

The king might think he was in the presence of a madwoman but what he would be experiencing is 'mirroring'. This is the term used for the way counsellors interpret their clients' (qv) feelings by imitating their expressions and echoing their words. He would wonder why. It would have to be explained to him that, like everything else in a consumer society, emotions can be bought. *Counselling* is a form of shopping – not for goods, but for emotions. The counsellor is an emotional mannequin, a superior form of shop assistant, slipping on smiles of sympathy, grins, looks of grief, and fragments of sentences so the customer can pick one to suit the moment. When a sale is made, called a 'closure', the counsellor wraps the emotion in a bogus explanation, ties it with psychobabble and hands it to the customer. Most customers come back. Emotions so easily purchased quickly wear out.

How much are new emotions? They are bought by the hour. An hour of grief work – simulated regret at the passing of a dog, cat, bank balance or husband – will set you back about £50, about the price of a contract on somebody's life on the streets of Moscow. King Rehoboam, on learning this, would, one hopes, summon the hosts of Midian.

MYLES HARRIS

CRIMINAL
One who wants the benefits of law for himself while depriving others (his victims) of the same. Formerly 'outlaw'. Usage note: as a word of Saxon origin, meaning 'fugitive from the law', outlaw describes one who has freely chosen to violate eternal moral principles. *Criminal*, by contrast, has a Latin root, which gives it a more technical connotation, and is thus better suited to modern notions of genetic and environmental determinism, as well as to the current rejection of permanent moral norms.

DANIEL LAPIN

CRITICAL
Left-wing (qv) and irrationally anti-capitalist, as in '*critical* theory', '*critical* philosophy' or '*critical* sociology', all of which are in a *critical* condition. Bears no relationship to criticism, ie the sceptical examination of factual evidence or logical connections with the purpose of getting

closer to the truth. The noun 'critique', now used vacuously as a verb, is normally substituted for criticize.

CHRISTIE DAVIES

CULTURAL STUDIES
The vacuous pondering the absent.

DAVID WOMERSLEY

CULTURE (I)
Mistakenly believed by Matthew Arnold to denote 'the best that has been thought and said', now in our modern way of speaking happily broadened to embrace those qualities and activities so much more prevalent amongst us, to wit the transient, the gross, the obscene, the pert, the criminal, the trivial, the impious, the shallow, the offensive, the mediocre, the banal, the perverse, the mercenary, the heinous, the strident, the unnatural, and the dull.

DAVID WOMERSLEY

CULTURE (II)
Britain, like many European countries, is now blessed with a Department of *Culture*. Let us hope that the Department will never be asked to address the problems of corporate *culture*, the *culture* of dependency or, for that matter, horticulture. Let us pray that it does not become dazzled by high *culture*, low *culture* and multi-*culture*. Above all, let us beseech the worthy inhabitants of the Department to form for themselves some purpose more clearly defined than is likely to emerge from the application of this term.

Once upon a time *culture*, in its abstract sense, meant the soil in which the mind grows. Then, it had a useful role to play in the language and a connection with its own linguistic roots. Now, it has become a deracinated voyager through the linguistic ether, vaguely alighting on a medley of shared practices, shared views, shared beliefs, shared preferences, shared origins

and shared traits – share, and ye shall be cultivat-
ed. Faced with such a circumstance, what should
we, the users of the language do? We can hardly
petition the august Department for the abolition
of the term. We do not have an Académie
Anglaise to which to apply for the word to enter
a proscribed list. We have, in short, not merely a
'*cultural* gap' and a '*cultural* divide', but also a
democratic deficit and an irresoluble linguistic
crisis. Alas, we can do no more than stand on
Dover Beach and listen to the melancholy, long
withdrawing roar.
OLIVER LETWIN

C ZAR

I think it began with the drugs Czar; then
there was a traffic Czar, followed by several
hospital-waiting-list Czars. At this rate we have
more Czars in Britain than the Romanovs. It is
axiomatic in public life that when politicos
start talking military language like 'task force',
'supremo', or 'quasi-royal' terminology, they
have just 'launched' (qv) another dud.
FREDERICK FORSYTH

D EATH

*Editor's note: Under this heading we include
an entry which illustrates several changed meanings.* When a young female dies, she is described
in the popular press as having had a 'bubbly'
personality. Should she have expired in an
unforeseen accident (qv) it is said that something
has gone 'horribly wrong'. People will leave 'flo-
ral tributes' at the scene. Should she have been
driven to take her own life by continuous bullying, her consequent loss of 'self-esteem' (qv) will
be mentioned and someone will say that had the
leading bully and his 'cohorts' been challenged
they 'may' have desisted. The papers will add
that although the ranks of the police have been
'decimated', their inaction in the matter 'begs
the question'. What has gone (horribly) wrong?

'Self-esteem' means vanity. The out-moded 'self-respect' at least implies the existence of some deserving qualities. A 'cohort' is 'a body of from 300 to 600 infantry, a tenth part of a Legion'. 'May/might' is a slippery one but the incorrect use leaps out of the page. 'Decimated' means 'to select by lot and put to death one of every ten'. And 'begging the question' is 'assuming the truth of the matter in dispute'. The police might ask the suspect in the matter of the dead girl 'Why did you kill her?'. Why are 'bunches of flowers' apparently considered vulgar and, in passing, how can a lawn – than which anything less like a hand or fingernails is hard to imagine – be 'manicured'.

ALICE THOMAS ELLIS

DECOMMISSIONING

What are we to make of this inflated and grandiose expression when it is treated as if it were the possible task of the Irish Republican Army? Ceremonies of commissioning and *decommissioning* are, above all, dignified occasions. We imagine companies of guardsmen on immaculately-groomed horses. Perhaps the Queen herself is present. *Decommissioning* is a word simply not available to murderous gangs of thugs whose historic purposes and operations are devoted to killing innocent passers-by, people at worship and young children.

Of course, using the word of the IRA – which the British Government repeatedly does – is very useful to the terrorists for it lends dignity and respectability by association and connotation and it encourages the public to regard the IRA as some sort of regular army complete with a code of chivalry and bathed in honour.

PETER MULLEN

DEVELOPMENT

Used to mean when prefixed by 'economic', the raising of per capita incomes in poor countries. This, the left argued, identified *development* with mere growth, which need not lead to *development*: by which they meant that growth would not in itself lead to the egalitarian society they wished to create. Now with all sorts of prefixes like 'sustainable' (qv) being added, it has become an even mushier word to signify any type of economic, social (qv) and political outcomes of which one approves. For others it has meant unorthodox or special as in '*development* economics' as contrasted with the conventional economics of developing countries.

DEEPAK LAL

D EVELOPMENT AID

A system under which the poor in rich countries help to line the Swiss Bank accounts of the rich in poor countries. There is no known example of a country in receipt of such government-to-government transfers leaving the ranks of the less-developed.

JOHN BLUNDELL

D ISCRIMINATE, DISCRIMINATION

To *discriminate* used to mean to observe a difference. One could, unfavourably, *discriminate* against someone or something. But to observe distinctions carefully was obviously a good thing. So if A and B were different, especially if they were subtly or finely different, to observe that difference was clearly a positive achievement. Thus the 'discriminating' person is congratulated by the Concise Oxford Dictionary of 1929 as being 'discerning, acute'.

Today people are found 'guilty' of *discrimination*. The worst sorts are racial *discrimination*, sexual *discrimination* and, increasingly, what is called *discrimination* on the grounds of sexual orientation. For instance, to prefer a person of one race to another for a job appointment where the person discarded was as well or better qualified than the person given the job would be viewed as bad behaviour and *'discriminatory'*. It is indeed bad behaviour, being both unfair to the candidates and denying the employing organization the best person for the job. But the behaviour is not bad because it is 'discriminatory' in the original sense. In fact it is bad because it is not *'discriminatory'*. The person doing the appointing has not noticed the relevant subtle differences.

While there may indeed be no relevant differences among races when it comes to matters such as job appointments, this is not so obviously the case with sex differences. The policy of mixed sex wards in hospitals for instance, or that of using women in military combat are indeed 'non-*discriminatory'* in the traditional sense because they do not notice or obstinately refuse to acknowledge real and relevant differences. In the new sense they are, then, *'discriminatory'*.

Generally progressive persons do not like the idea of difference, especially in education. This is awkward since the ability to detect subtle distinctions could well be said to be a crucial part of education itself.

DIGBY ANDERSON

DISTANCE as in KEEPING ONE'S DISTANCE
The opposite of *keeping one's distance* was being familiar and, as the word suggests, familiar, intimate, unceremonious relationships were appropriate for one's family and friends. They were not appropriate to business and professional relations partly because these were not relations with friends, partly because they were relations with superiors and inferiors. When the patient consults his doctor, he is after superior knowledge and medical authority. This is not the place for Christian names. When a man becomes prime minister he takes on a superior social status. Christian names, and the rest of the terminology of intimate friendship, are not appropriate. It may be that those who oppose distance and formality in any circumstance as

stilted and stuffy also claim to oppose relationships of inequality. But such a claim is not borne out by their behaviour. They themselves accept the unequal salaries that go with their jobs and seek the unequal competence of doctors and other professionals. To use intimate forms in such situations is to fake intimacy.
DIGBY ANDERSON

DIVERSITY

The property of differing in any respect (especially in race, gender or sexuality), other than in commitment to a liberal progressive social (qv) agenda. The term is usually used in reference to a group whose members so differ. However, by extension, it may refer to an individual characteristic, as in the case of a Harvard undergraduate who, when students were asked to list on an index card what they considered their virtues, wrote: 'I am diverse'. As a virtue, *diversity* bears the peculiar advantages of needing to be neither acquired nor practised, but merely possessed, and of being immediately available to anyone (at least anyone who does not live an unassuming or traditional life without ambitions to expand the limits of body-piercing).

Its status as a virtue may be seen in its role in the education of the young. Whereas formerly historical and fictional figures were considered worthy of attention as exemplars of virtues such as courage, justice, honesty or patriotism, students' attention is now directed to figures and practices that exemplify *diversity*. Naturally a characteristic of democratic orders because of their high degree of personal freedom, *diversity* attains its pre-eminent status as a virtue in modern liberal democracy. There it serves to palliate the tedium of homogenization and mediocritization attendant upon egalitarian social conditions, and the emptying of character attendant upon liberal abstract individualism and mass media.
MARK SHIFFMAN

ELITISM

This term is derived from the French élire – to choose or select – and denotes the theory and/or practice of those who emphasize the role and importance (either for themselves or others) of groups that are deemed to be chosen as 'best' within a specified field. It also implies that such elites enjoy their superiority and benefit therefrom.

Such usage is descriptive. It leaves open the grounds or attributes on which such choices are (or have been) based. It also leaves open whether, in any specific country, entry into its elites is closed (ie controlled by a ruling party) or pluralist.

In modern parlance the term has become what the philosophers used to call a boo-word in contrast to such hurrah-words as egalitarianism. It is largely pejorative: people are very unwilling to describe themselves as elitist. This ideological usage goes well beyond the sensible recognition that pride in superior knowledge, intelligence or skills, (and more generally inherited advantages) may indeed be excessive or disagreeable.

It is a weapon for those who on moral or political grounds are fighting against inequalities, privileges and traditions. It fits in very well with post-modernist doctrines that deny that objective knowledge is possible: claims to such objectivity are deemed part of an order of inequality (qv) imposed by power-holders based on class, gender or race. This is thought to be especially obnoxious under 'capitalism' (qv) – despite evidence that political, functional and artistic elites also evolve under 'socialism'.

The anti-elitist position, like other forms of idealism, also merges with the politics of envy – not least in matters of educational provision. Here the cry of 'elitist' (and its brother-cry of 'divisive') has been used to oppose (and, where possible, remove) programmes that would discriminate (qv) in favour of, for example, specially gifted children – not to mention the private education sector.

There are signs that educational anti-*elitism* has begun a retreat in Britain – but its advocates remain determined and influential. They see no irony in the fact that they are themselves a self-perpetuating elite fuelled by a sense of guilt and an appetite for power over others.
JULIUS GOULD

ENVIRONMENT

Environner in French means 'to surround' so the *environment* is simply our surroundings. The word began to develop something like its modern meaning with the rise of Darwinian biology (and the greater chance of a species surviving if it is adapted to its *environment*) and as a translation of the German geographers' Umwelt. From about 1850 to 1950, an 'environmentalist' was one who believed in the primacy of surrounding conditions (as opposed to genetics or free will) in the causation of human affairs; this position is now covered by the phrase 'environmental determinism'.

However, in the second half of the twentieth century, 'environmentalist' was used mainly to describe people who sought to 'preserve' or 'conserve' their surroundings. The focus of their efforts might be local and architectural ('urban conservation') at one extreme, or global and ecological at the other.

The danger of talking about 'the *environment*' is that it is so often and easily treated theomorphically. Thus people easily step into talking about 'the needs (qv)' of the *environment* and judging actions and practices as to whether they are 'environmentally friendly'. As the *environment* is literally everything (note the slogan that 'man is *environment* to man') this amounts to a kind of pantheism. It is usually also a kind of ethical trump card which gives authoritarian rights to its bearer. In one of the most popular works of environmentalism, Jonathon Porritt's Seeing Green, the author insists that, although he believes in freedom in many respects, all human beings must conform to 'the needs of a finite planet' (which, presumably, he will be allowed to define). Thus 'the *environment*' represents, in many arguments, the principles or interests (qv) of someone who wishes to impose their will upon you.

To be fair to 'the *environment*' it is often a counter-weight to 'the market' which is a concept with very similar properties.

LINCOLN ALLISON

E QUALITY (I)

As in 'the policies of our party are designed to promote *equality* and social (qv) justice (qv).' The history of *equality* as a political ideal began with the assertion in the American Declaration of Independence of the supposedly self-evident truth 'that all men are created equal'. But that phrase was not followed by a full-stop. The Signers were not asserting, and most certainly did not believe, either that all human beings are equally talented or even that talents are distributed across all human subsets in the same proportions. Instead the Signers specified the dimension in which they believed us all to be equal. It was in our natural endowment with 'certain inalienable rights', among which are 'life, liberty and the pursuit' – but not the provision of any means necessary to achieve – 'happiness'.

The *equality* proclaimed by the French Revolution of 1789 was an *equality* in the status of citizens as such. It involved *la carrière ouverte aux talents*, or what we should now call *equality* of opportunity (qv). Because individuals differ both in their talents and in so many other ways, *equality* of opportunity is bound to lead to inequalities of outcome. And, in so far as people strive to achieve excellence in various fields, these manifold differences between individuals are bound to result in elites consisting of the most excellent in those fields. (Even the most Procrustean of egalitarians must nevertheless want the members of the teams which they support to constitute such an elite!)

The promotion of the kinds of *equality* identified with social justice is always taken to embrace *equality* before the law and equality of opportunity. But the only outcome which these equalisers want to equalize is, paradoxically, that of incomes. Their aim is an ever greater but, for practical if no other reasons, never complete *equality* of incomes.

ANTONY FLEW

EQUALITY (II)

Half the workforce want *equality*; the rest want greater differentials.

CHARLES GOODSON-WICKES

ETHICS

The largely ignored universal principles of right and wrong that should govern human action, because they promote the virtues (ie excellences) necessary for the flourishing of that which is distinctively human; see Aristotle, The Nicomachean Ethics.

Once widely recognized, these principles are now generally doubted, in part because of the scepticism that has afflicted philosophy since Descartes. Suffering from an inadequate metaphysics, which leaves all knowledge and human action profoundly ungrounded, most modern philosophers misguidedly believe that ethical absolutes cannot be justified.

Because they lack an adequate metaphysics, both of the most prominent modern ethical theories – Utilitarianism and Kantian deontology – are conspicuously unable to give satisfactory accounts of ordinary ethical judgments. If (counter-factually) being good simply means acting so as to maximize utility, or acting in a way that is universalizable, most common ethical judgments cannot be justified. Justice, for example, is reduced to mere prudence or procedure; there is no room for the notions of merit and desert that are commonly and rightly associated with the term. Equally, such theories cannot accommodate the fact that context is relevant to moral judgements without reducing *ethics* to relativism or consequentialism.

Because both Utilitarianism and deontology are so obviously unsatisfactory, it is often concluded that philosophical *ethics* has nothing to do with 'real life'. As guides for action, people often revert to equally (but less obviously) unsatisfactory bases for making ethical decisions. The Golden Rule (treat others as you would be treated) will not do: applied by a masochist, it would (incorrectly) suggest that inflicting unnecessary pain on everyone was ethically right. Equally, although recommended by most world religions, altruism cannot be the basis for morality. Merely preferring another's interests to one's own does not and cannot make an action good: in the absence of some other, independent criterion, preferring the other's interests (those of a sadist, for example) might well lead to actions that are wrong.

ELAINE STERNBERG

E THNIC (I)

To be *ethnic* used to mean to possess the characteristic of a nation or particular group within the nation. Now it means to be black (qv). Other smaller groups within our society – Asians, Welsh and Cornish people – sometimes lay claim to the title, but they must not be allowed to get away with it. If you're black, you're *ethnic*. If you're not black, you're not *ethnic*.

AUBERON WAUGH

ETHNIC (II)

Until the close of the Second World War, most people felt free to talk or write about 'race', and the supposed characteristics of different races without much restriction. Among the white races, the overall superiority of the white races was assumed by almost everybody.

The Nazi theory and practice of racialism put a stop to that. They made 'race' itself a dirty word among liberal thinkers, for whom the absolute equality of all races in all respects became one of the most cherished (and most unsound) of their articles of faith. The word 'race' could still be heard, of course, among the common people, in spite of official disapproval and even legal penalties.

A more remote word of Greek origin, free from the taint of Nazi evil and with a nice scientific ring, was a welcome substitute. So *ethnic* with its pseudo-scientific derivatives ('ethnicity' and '*ethnic* identity' are popular among archaeologists) swept the board.

Unfortunately *ethnic* has found its way into the unlettered 'media' and into common speech, with often grotesque results. It is taken to mean simply 'non-white', as in 'the *ethnic* minorities' and even 'the *ethnic* community', taken to include all non-white people.

Ethnic has thus acquired some of the 'discriminatory' or 'racist' feeling that liberal thinkers so desperately wished to avoid. I have never actually heard it used among the unregenerate as a term of abuse. But I have seen a graffito: 'Ethnics Out!' Truly the work of liberal thinkers is never done.

MICHAEL WHARTON

EVIL

In traditional metaphysics, moral *evil* is understood to be the privation of good, the relative absence of the fullness of divinely-created being. Thus, *evil* could not be a real, personal force from without, but a willful falling short on the part of responsible individuals. Physical *evil*, such as natural disasters, is understood to be real and painful but accidental, except insofar as such occasions become the opportunity to endure suffering and align oneself with divine providence. Ultimately, the hatred the *evil* have of the good is held to be a fundamentally mysterious datum of the human condition. How one could reconcile the occurrence of *evil* with a benevolent, omnipotent God is generally referred to as theodicy, or 'the problem of *evil*'.

In contemporary usage, however, the 'problem' of evil – when it is not explained away altogether – is put in abstract and adjectival rather than substantive terms. *Evil* is usually cast as 'structural' or 'social' *evil*, qualified in impersonal terms and only rarely attributed to a concrete human personality. Social *evils* are synonymous with social ills more generally for which there are putative solutions. Evil as a mystery of the human soul is replaced with abstract causal reductions: upbringing, social and economic contexts, mores and discrimination (qv). On this understanding, *evil* is an abstract, impersonal, and external force which acts upon largely helpless victims (qv). At the same time, there is an intense personification of *evil*. Hitler is the paradigm of *evil* – more so, suspiciously, than Mao or Stalin – but even Hitler's *evil* derives, it seems, from pathetic maladjustments of self-esteem (qv).

Evil actions tend to be a source of shock and surprise, as though the progress of material prosperity had somehow eradicated that lust for destruction which lurks in every human soul. Massacres, torture, and other *evil* acts have ceased to cast us back upon (allegedly outdated) metaphysical concerns – *evil* is no longer mysterious, it is simply unintelligible in the modern psychological idiom. The problem of *evil*, it would appear, is no longer God's problem, but nor is it quite our own; we see and hear no *evil* if we are

convinced *evil* resides in our environment and not in the depths of the human soul.
TODD BREYFOGLE

EXCELLENCE

If *excellence* has to do with excelling, it is a comparative term. By definition, not everything can be excellent. And, on the principle that a good wine needs no bush, or just in virtue of good manners, those institutions which are really excellent need not advertise the fact. By implication, then, anything which proclaims itself as excellent is probably not, and by definition not all our children can go to excellent schools. 'Promoting *excellence* for everyone', then, is an incoherent goal, which only a society of edgy and incoherent mediocrity could espouse. But then, in most cases *excellence* has now become indistinguishable from mediocrity.
ANTHONY O'HEAR

EXCLUSION

The older dictionaries are neutral on *exclusion*. It means shutting out and there can be good and bad reasons for shutting someone out. Recently, 'social *exclusion*' (qv) has been announced by the Government to be a bad thing, an unmitigated evil (qv). Indeed, a Unit (qv) has been set up to get rid of it. Why has social *exclusion* been accepted as an evil? The first odd thing about it is that the same chaps who are against social *exclusion* are for community (qv) and there is nothing like communities, especially tightly knit communities, when it comes to a spot of excluding. Country villages are one example, so are mining communities and gentlemen's clubs. But so too are gatherings of young people. Youth (qv) is also admired by the anti-exclusionists: try muscling in on some park or pub they have colonized. The anti-country measures initiated by urban activists against country communities are an interesting instance of anti-exclusionists trying to exclude, even ban, ways of life they dislike.

Communities are groups of people who share traditions, residence, interests, affections, languages. The extent to which they are bound together is the extent to which they are set apart from people not in the community. Those who favour 'diversity' (qv) and community might ask themselves whether this does not often imply support for *exclusion*.

The *exclusion* debate used to be called the social mobility debate. The same assumption was made then that social immobility, the lack of movement of the children of fathers in one occupation to an occupation with higher or lower rewards and status was a bad thing. Such children were being kept out or excluded. High social mobility was a good thing. But high social mobility can destroy community, breaking attachments, settledness and traditions.

It can be argued against the current assumptions that, overall, exclusion is probably a good thing. It testifies to the solidity of diverse communities. If anything, modern society could do with a bit more exclusion, especially in the ostracism of criminals and other deviants.

The left (qv), of course, have one particular group in mind when they talk of the socially excluded. They mean low income, especially unemployed families. There they may have a point. But in a competition to find the most unfairly excluded group, surely smokers would win. And the same people who have set up a unit to get rid of *exclusion* for low-income families have set up another to increase the *exclusion* of smokers.

DIGBY ANDERSON

E XCLUSION as in SOCIAL EXCLUSION
Once upon a time, people were 'poor'. Today they are 'socially excluded'.

To describe somebody as 'poor' is to use a neutral term, it leaves open the question of who or what is responsible for their situation. To describe somebody as 'socially excluded', however, is to use a loaded term. Social exclusion is something that happens to people. People are victims (qv) of *social exclusion*.

The idea of *social exclusion* originated in France, but it was soon taken up by the left (qv) in Britain. New Labour's chief guru, Peter Mandelson, explained in 1997: '*Social exclusion*... (was) the poison that seeped through the Thatcher years and corroded our society.'

One of New Labour's first initiatives when it assumed office in 1997 was the establishment of a '*Social Exclusion* Unit'. It produces reports. It is concerned about 'What can happen when people or areas suffer from a combination of linked problems such as unemployment (qv), poor skills, low incomes, poor housing, high crime environments, bad health, poverty (qv) and family breakdown.'

The essential point about this language is that individuals 'suffer' social exclusion; they never never bring it upon themselves. If somebody is 'excluding' you, it can hardly be your fault. If you play truant from school, it is the schooling system that is failing. If you do not have a job, it is because employment opportunities (qv) have been denied you.

A Junior Minister in the Labour Government, summed this up in a speech in 1999. 'Those of us here today are lucky,' she said, 'because we fortunately do not suffer the debilitating impact of *social exclusion*.' Social exclusion is thus like a random hailstorm; some of us get hit, others somehow miraculously dodge it.

Social exclusion is Third Way (qv) Speak for poverty. Its attraction is its implication that poverty can never be the fault of those who are poor.
PETER SAUNDERS

FASCISM, FASCIST

Strictly speaking, designates the political movement so named and headed by the interwar Italian dictator Benito Mussolini, but extensible to others like it. The name derives from the fasces, the bundles of rods and axes carried before Ancient Roman magistrates as a symbol of State authority. Mussolini's ideology was a cocktail of Marxism, Darwinism, Sorelian irrationalism, and Italian Futurism. Added to this was an inverted Hegelianism devised by the philosopher Gentile, under which institutions superficially resembling those of representative government were in fact used to hand down orders from above (as they were also by the Bolshevik dictator Lenin – admired by Mussolini – who referred to them as 'transmission belts').

Mussolini's regime, though violent, theatrical and authoritarian (besides being, in the opinion of many spectators, vulgar and absurd), was not wholly totalitarian. Some autonomous institutions survived, albeit often in greatly attenuated form (eg law). Mussolini made a concordat with the Pope (thus recognizing the rights and power of the Roman Catholic Church), while the King remained as head of state (he eventually dismissed Mussolini). The regime was also (until Mussolini's ally Hitler demanded anti-Jewish measures) not notably racist. Its ideal was the classical, ethnically ecumenical, pseudo-Roman State rather than, as under German National Socialism, the mystical, romanticised, 'pure-blooded' Volk. For all that, and despite other significant differences (especially in the sheer scale of their crimes), it may be thought excusable, if somewhat loose, to refer to National Socialism also as *fascist*.

What is not excusable is the rhetorical trick, once fashionable among Communists and the 'hard' left generally, and still not obsolete, of tarring everything disapproved of with the *fascist* brush. The object is, by demonising it, to put beyond discussion or even contemplation (ie beyond intellectual temptation) whatever is perceived as an obstacle to left-wing interests and projects. Thus conservatism, liberalism, markets and capitalism, education, religion, normality (eg 'heterosexism') and even language have all been described (the last by Roland Barthes) as *fascist*. What they have in common is the diffuse, 'natural' (qv) or customary authority which attaches to consensual arrangements and a cultural inheritance, and which must therefore conflict, both with the left's primitive anarchistic yearnings for 'liberation', and with the concentrated, top-down, systematic and non-negotiable power which the left actually (and by contrast) requires in order to effect its promised wholesale social transformations.

If the latter power should appear indistinguishable from that of *fascism*, this should occasion no surprise, for *fascism* learnt its political manners from its older mentor and rival, communism, having over it the sole advantage (if it was an advantage) of being more honest about its true goal, viz. the exercise of power for its own sake. This also explains why *fascist* is (or was) a left-wing boo-word, since the deep community of interest between these rival ideologies, together with *fascism's* comparative openness about the fact, needs at all costs to be dissembled.
ROBERT GRANT

FATHER

Inseminator of women and male parent of child or children. Once conception has taken place, his duties are over. Further contact with the inseminated woman is eschewed, unless money is needed or sex desired, or the relief of feelings by violence (qv) becomes necessary. In exceptional circumstances, a *father* may go halves in the purchase of new shoes for the child, and will then consider himself something of a martyr. The *father* tends to subscribe to a male fertility cult, and therefore inseminates as many women as possible. On the other hand, he may try to procure a miscarriage by kicking mother in the abdomen while she is pregnant: an abortive action, as it were.

THEODORE DALRYMPLE

FORMALITY

In the West, according to its enemies, a 'bourgeois' (qv) type of human behaviour. Formality pertains to the organization of interpersonal conduct such that it transforms the experience of the physical presence of others into a communion of minds and souls. *Formality* in interpersonal relations involves the use of a repertoire of procedures, gestures and verbal expressions which constitute shared conceptions of the person and of the good life. Access to such patterns of behaviour is access to civilisation.

In the cities of Paris and New York, and the State of California, *formality* has come under severe criticisms and many attempts have been made to replace *formality* with informality. Informality is praised for advancing social equality (qv) and for allowing unmeditated, ad hoc, spontaneous communication and self-expression (qv), states of being which are highly valued among certain intellectual circles. These intellectuals wish to deprive the rest of us of the type of disciplined reasoning and deliberate pursuit of common objectives from which they themselves have benefited, apparently to the point of satiation.

In actual fact, informality causes the regression of human life into the primal state of flux, chaos and indifference. Informality is being applied everywhere: from informal dress, to informal job interviews, informal lectures and seminars (qv), and informal board meetings. We shall soon have Informal Thought, Informal Love (vide the new concept of 'coupling and uncoupling'), Informal Godhead and Informal Existence which is no existence at all.

The cult of Informality is the glorification of laziness and unpreparedness. It endorses thoughtlessness and neglect of duty towards others. Critics of *Formality* as a component of life with others do not wish to replace particular forms of human contact with other forms, but wish to destroy all forms, all human institutions and with them destroy all patterns of commitment and expectation as 'mere *formality*'.

ATHENA S LEOUSSI

FORTITUDE

A ridiculous quality, as a consequence of which people bottle up their feelings and therefore become emotionally disturbed many years later, for which the only cure is intensive counselling (qv).

THEODORE DALRYMPLE

FRATERNITY

A social (qv) category made popular by the French Revolution (*Liberté, Egalité, Fraternité*). *Fraternity* goes beyond equality because it establishes that men are so deeply related to each other that everyone has a right (qv) to his fair share of the goods legitimately owned by others. These goods may be represented by material as well as by spiritual goods. In the nineteenth century, a strong accent was put on the spiritual side. It was *fraternity* which kept united people of different social classes in the distress of war, natural catastrophes, social unrest. The very existence of a nation rested on the existence of the sense of *fraternity* among all its citizens. All this has gone now. The spiritual side of *fraternity* is forgotten, Even in France nobody speaks any more of *fraternity*, but everyone talks of 'solidarity', which is just another name for income redistribution.

ANGELO M PETRONI

FRIENDSHIP

A case of long-term, now terminal decline. Once – a very long time ago – *friendship* was of the same as or greater importance than marriage (qv) and recognized as a moral state (Aristotle, Cicero, Aquinas, Montaigne, Jeremy Taylor, Boswell). Even the nineteenth-century Newman saw love of friends and relations as the start of Christian love and a 'special test of virtue'. And as recently as 50 years ago, C S Lewis could remember it as 'the happiest and most fully human of loves'. The virtues associated with this high notion of *friendship* were honesty, especially frankness of speech, loyalty, trust, self-sacrifice and permanence of character – *friendships* were built on the virtue of constancy.

Friends brought out the best in each other; they were other selves. Now friends are hardly distinguishable from mates or occasional companions, persons to drink lager with on Friday evenings or with whom to compare notes about hairdressers; people speak of new friends they met the previous weekend.

Once *friendship*, because it was a morally based relationship, could play a public role in politics and business. *Friendships* though not made for political and material advantage could be the subsequent source of it and quite properly so. Now business and politics are obsessed with equal rights and transparency (qv). Poor old *friendship* being confidential and preferential, is hence to be driven out of both as croneyism and the old boys' network. It is now a relationship confined to trivial recreation, a source of fun and exacting few and passing obligations.

DIGBY ANDERSON

FRIGHTENING

In the 1980s this was automatically applied to any form of self-defence by the West, or anything done or said by Mr Reagan or Mrs Thatcher. With the Cold War over, it has simply become a standard word of disapproval (though *de rigeur* when mentioning, eg the Orange Order in Ulster). The Observer recently said the price of CDs was *frightening*.

JOHN MALONEY

G ENDER

Term appropriated from the study of grammar by feminists, in order to describe that aspect of sexual behaviour and sexual identity which is 'socially constructed'. By replacing the word 'sex' with the word *gender*, wherever sex is being discussed, the feminists hope to create the impression that the sexual aspect of the human being is infinitely plastic, and can be remodelled to any specification. Hence we can free ourselves of the existing '*gender* roles', which allegedly make women subservient to men. So successful has this piece of brain-washing been, that application forms for a passport now ask applicants for their *gender* – meaning their sex. If the feminists were right, you could honestly reply 'don't know' or 'working on it'.

ROGER SCRUTON

G ENOCIDE

Subs. *genocidal* adj. (L *genus*, Gr *Genos*, people or naturally generated class, L *caedere*, kill). 1944. The attempt to destroy all members of an abstractly specified set of people This was most commonly a racial or national group, but the word has dangerously expansive tendencies. The powerful rhetorical appeal of this term derives from the Nazi attempt to eliminate Jews and Gypsies in Europe during the Second World War, but the idea has been extended since. In 1951 the United Nations issued its Convention on the Prevention and Punishment of the Crime of Genocide, in which *genocide* came to cover a remarkably wide number of public policies, such as 'killing members of the group' and 'causing serious bodily or mental harm' to them. The UN definition goes beyond the etymology in defining the crime as any of a set of acts 'committed with intent to destroy, in whole or in part, a national, ethnical, racial or religious group as such...'. 'Gay Lib' activists are inclined to include hostile treatment of homosexuals as genocidal. Measures intended to prevent births within the group were included in the Convention, a clause which might make Indian and Chinese birth control policies genocidal. Transferring children of one group to another group was also included in the UN definition, a clause which suggested that Australian adoption policies earlier in the twentieth century, in which half-caste children were taken into fostering by white families, or into orphanages, might constitute *genocide*.

The legal significance of *genocide* is that it is an international crime *par excellence*, and it appeals to political activists because it transfers any such allegation out of national jurisdictions into the glare of international publicity. Article VIII authorises any Contracting Party to call upon the United Nations to take action for the prevention and suppression of *genocide*. The crime is in part constituted by the intent to achieve the elimination of any relevant group. The range of uses for the term may be illustrated by the fact that the repressions of Augusto Pinochet in Chile after the revolution of 1973 were implausibly described as *genocide* in the 1998 writ of a Spanish magistrate demanding Pinochet's extradition from Great Britain.

The charge of *genocide* is commonly used by indigenous or tribal peoples demanding rights (qv) against national governments in Western liberal democracy.

The range of the term can be seen in Article IIIc of the UN Convention which includes 'Direct and public incitement to commit *genocide*'.

KENNETH MINOGUE

GENTLEMAN

An historical character whose native habitat was (and still is?) England; recognized as such from Chaucer to Evelyn Waugh. Arnold reported a total absence in France; Hippolyte Taine, a Frenchman, agreed. Coleridge insisted, similarly, that the species was unknown in Germany; Huber, a German, concurred. Now commonly, and wrongly, believed to have been one defined by birth, heraldic status or entitlement to bear arms ('Though he be a lord, he is not a gentleman'). More accurately, and throughout English history, understood as one with the appearance, manners and virtues worthy of the title: elegant and yet proper, even simple, in dress; self-assured and yet agreeable, even accommodating, in social relations; truthful and yet tactful, principled without being priggish, courageous in the cause of justice, generous on behalf of the weak, capable of lasting indignation at the expense of the wicked. Valued by Victorian radicals from Samuel Smiles to Mr Gladstone, who understood his civilising potentialities. Increasingly derided by their twentieth-century successors who acknowledge only his seeming anachronistic vices. And dismissed by contemporary feminists who take him to be a contradiction in terms. The latter may, as much through their own efforts as in the perspicacity of their observations, eventually be proved right. The former might recall Taine's observation that: unlike the French *gentilhomme*, English gentlemen have not become...ornamental parasites but rather administrators, patrons, promoters of reforms and good managers of the commonwealth... well-educated men who apply themselves to work and who...are...the most useful...citizens ...of the whole nation. Either that, or they might compare the present membership of the House of Lords with what is often referred to as (I)nternational (W)hite (T)rash.

SIMON GREEN

G REEN

People began to call themselves and behaviour *green*, or not, some time in the mid 1970s, though Greenpeace's use of the word, and its use to describe ecologism's forays into politics pre-date that. To be *green* is to believe oneself guided by ecological principles, and to believe that society at large is insufficiently so guided. *Greens* normally seek to 'enlarge the circle of empathy', that is, to extend the moral realm beyond the human, and towards animals, plants and the planet generally.

Green ecologism (importantly this is a narrow sub-set of real ecological thinking) emphasizes that natural systems are fragile, stable and full of communities (and are thus like socialist Utopias) as opposed to their being robust, dynamic and opportunistic (like the free market or human society). Both pictures have elements of the truth.

More recently, great corporations have sought to be *green*, but their efforts are derided as greenwash by many of those who hold to older usages which enshrine ideas of dissidence, radicalism, decentralization, and (to use the neologism of Ivan Illich) de-institutionalisation.

RICHARD D NORTH

H ANDICAPPED

A condition providing advantage to the individual to whom it is imputed. A golfer, for example, enjoys a 'handicap' that makes it possible to win a tournament against the best players. In this way, *handicapped* persons are said to 'overcome' their 'handicaps'. Except in golf and in some other sports, horseracing for example, the term has fallen into disuse, because the *handicapped* have generally been eradicated from society through the magic of language. The helping professions have transformed all handicaps into conditions of 'challenge' – the physically, mentally, vertically and variously 'challenged'. Politicians and lawyers have also informed the *handicapped* that they have been denied their equal rights (qv) because of their disabilities, so that they now belong to the same class as women and minorities.

GRAEME NEWMAN

H EALTHY

Taking risks by smoking, being a couch potato, or eating butter has become not just stupid, but sinful. The *healthy* eschew tobacco, eat nuts, jog every day, and are allowed a glass of red wine at the weekend. For doctors, health is the absence of disease so that the only *healthy* are the inadequately investigated. Life itself, being a universally fatal, sexually transmitted disease, should be enjoyed to the full. Perhaps being *healthy* should be defined as coping with the 'slings and arrows of outrageous fortune'. This has many advantages. It permits health to those who have to cope with disability and even allows the possibility of dying *healthy*. As Theodore Fox remarked, 'Life itself is not the most important thing in life. Some cling to it as a miser to his money and to as little purpose. Some risk it for a song, a hope, a cause, for wind in their hair.'

JAMES McCORMICK

H ELL

(Archaic) A place of eternal torment as punishment, in the life to come, for impiety and injustice while on Earth. These gruesome torments, in contrast with the eternal bliss of heavenly paradise, were understood not metaphorically but as the real physical consequences of a life of sin.

In contemporary usage, the meaning of *hell* has changed in accordance with changing beliefs about heaven and increasing disbelief in the concept of sin. Ever-accurate social scientific surveys show that more people believe in heaven than believe in God, while increasingly few believe in hell at all. At the same time, as people embrace a vision of heaven on earth, *hell* takes on material, earthly trappings, connoting not punishment but intense (and often undeserved) physical or mental suffering. In the relative absence of a notion of sin, enduring earthly *hell* is not unavoidable punishment for evil. Rather, *hell* is understood to be suffering imposed unjustly by others and therefore a state of affairs which demands an enforced amelioration by some third party, often a government agency or international non-governmental organization. Thus, *hell* has been separated from traditional notions of justice or desert. Needless to say, if *hell* did exist as a place, its population would be small. Indeed, divine mercy, on this popular view, would not permit anyone to be damned by divine justice, save for the problematic case of Hitler and possibly Margaret Thatcher.

'Hell' is frequently applied metaphorically to any unpleasantness, however trivial, as is typical with many words which properly denote only extreme conditions or events. So, *hell* is most commonly used in phrases such as 'so and so makes my life a living *hell*' or simply, 'go to *hell*'. There are further figurative usages – '*hell* on wheels' and 'raising *hell*' – where *hell* may serve as a term of approbation, celebrating irresponsibility and mayhem. Sartre of course famously wrote that '*hell* is other people'. This may well be true, but then again these people are living, likely to be given subsidies irrespective of merit, and are destined for heaven, whatever their sins may be.

TODD BREYFOGLE

H EREDITARY PRINCIPLE

Currently declared to be unmodern and unacceptable in such cases as *hereditary* peers sitting and voting in the House of Lords. It is not, however, obsolete. The very persons who declare

it to be so for peers and perhaps the monarchy make much use of it for themselves when announcing that this generation of Britons, Imperialists and industrialists should compensate the descendants of slaves, exploited third world persons and victims (qv) of century-old industrial pollution for the sins of their great grandfathers.
DIGBY ANDERSON

HISTORIC

Regularly misapplied by the media to mean 'we think this is very important'. No new initiative in the Northern Ireland peace process is ever promoted without this adjective applied, usually to describe the equally often misapplied noun 'breakthrough'. In fact four-fifths of events dubbed *historic* today will not in reality detain genuine historians at all in the future. The rule ought to be that historic is only ever applied to events which took place in the past, never in the present.
ANDREW ROBERTS

HOLOCAUST

Properly used the term *Holocaust* relates to the historical fact of Nazi Germany's systematic murder of six million Jews. It is now applied to anything of which the speaker disapproves (eg the '*Holocaust*' inflicted upon the planet by multinationals), thus trying to transfer some of the wholly justified horror at the crimes of the Nazis to the speaker's pet hate. *Holocaust* must now be one of the most abused words in modern English. As a description of the Nazi destruction of the Jews, it did not even enter the language until the 1960s. Barely 20 years ago, leading Jewish scholars were still complaining about the lack of discussion of the Holocaust in the West.

Now the *Holocaust* is everywhere. In Britain it is taught in the national school curriculum; universities offer degrees in *Holocaust* and genocide (qv) studies; and the New Labour

Government has announced a national *Holocaust* Remembrance Day. In America, where the *Holocaust* has become the stuff of Hollywood blockbusters, things have gone further still.

It seems that the more the *Holocaust* becomes history, the more it is in the news. The motives behind this fresh obsession with the Holocaust have to do with the present rather than the past. The *Holocaust* has been turned into a cheap political resource, to be exploited for dubious purposes.

The Nazi *Holocaust* has become perhaps the last moral absolute in an uncertain world. It seems ever-harder for those in authority to create a consensus (qv) about what is right and wrong on issues ranging from child-rearing to GM food. How comforting then, to be able to fall back on the *Holocaust* as one issue where all decent citizens can agree that there remains a clear line between Good and Evil (qv). And how convenient to be able to draw on the moral authority of the victims of the *Holocaust* in order to boost the claims of your own pet cause, by claiming that 'another *Holocaust*' is being caused by the motor car, or by AIDS, or even by battery chicken farming.

Investing in the *Holocaust* industry is largely an exercise in self-flattery for societies like Britain and the USA. Uncertain of what they stand for in the post -Cold War world, they have leapt anew at the chance to advertise their civilized virtues by contrasting them with Nazi barbarism. The *Holocaust* Museum in Washington DC highlights George Washington's assurance that the US government 'gives to bigotry no sanction, to persecution no assistance'. And the New Labour Government's proposal for a *Holocaust* Remembrance Day boasts that it will be a 'national focus for education', promoting our 'democratic and tolerant society, free of the evils of prejudice and racism'. The message is that we might not be too sure of who we are any more, but at least we know we're not Nazis.

The trend today is to discover new Nazis and fresh *Holocausts* in faraway places. Regional conflicts around the world are now routinely equated with the Nazi experience, by appropriating the language of genocide. There is a heavy price to pay for this exploitation of the *Holocaust*. It distorts our understanding of both the present and the past. For instance, once a people like the Serbs have been branded as the new Nazis, there is no need to understand the complexities of Balkan politics or the dangers of international intervention. By turning a political problem into a black and white moral issue, the *Holocaust*-mongers offer an excuse for ignorance.

Worse still, anything that suggests that the slaughter of six million Jews should be compared with today's local conflicts can only serve to belittle the unique horror of the *Holocaust* itself. There are two kinds of *Holocaust* revisionism today. There are a handful of people who deny that the slaughter of six million ever happened. And then there are people who, however worthy their intentions may be, are helping to rewrite the place of the *Holocaust* in history. By equating every civil war with the *Holocaust*, and by raising it in relation to every moral issue, they are in danger or rendering the barbarism of the Final Solution banal. When one hears eco-activists talking about a *Holocaust* of frogs, it is surely time to rescue it for history.

MICK HUME

H OMOPHOBIA

Generic term invented by 'gay' activists to denote social prejudice against homosexuals, personal revulsion at homosexuals, or opposition to full equality between homosexuals and heterosexuals. The word *homophobia* is cleverly designed to resemble a medical pathology or psychiatric disorder (eg agoraphobia, hydrophobia). This suggests that 'gay' militants, aware that homosexuality was once treated as a medical disorder, have taken revenge by pathologising prejudice. As a word, *homophobia* makes little linguistic sense, being derived from the Ancient Greek *homos*, same, and *phobia*, dread or horror. In modern (qv) English it should mean 'fear of the same' rather than prejudice against homosexuals. However, such linguistic niceties are of little importance to the post-1968 activist generation who support causes such as 'gay rights'. Since the early 1990s, *homophobia* has taken its place in the litany of political correctness, alongside 'racism' and 'sexism'. Ritual denunciations of these three evils are obligatory for any politician who wants to be considered 'modern' (qv), be he left (qv) or right (qv). This has three results: the silencing of most opponents of political correctness; the treatment of homosexuals, ethnic (qv) minority groups and women as voting fodder rather than individuals; and the myth (qv) that race, sex and sexual orientation are part of the same 'social question' rather than discrete issues. The concept of *homophobia* is part of a long-term strategy by 'gay' activists to win recognition as a quasi-ethnic group.

AIDAN RANKIN

H ONOUR (I)

Like many words, *honour* has fallen into disuse. It speaks of a pre-modern world guided by obligation and not by rights (qv). This world is best seen as being essentially chivalric, and turning on people's sense of duty to themselves, family, tribe and nation, which in turn demands loyalty (especially when one is being loyal to people and institutions behaving badly). One *honours* a cheque and debts, and this usage captures the discomfort *honour* almost always involves. An 'honourable' action is one in which one is upholding ideals set by society. One *honours* those who perform those duties. These actions might well be private and go unrecognized. But the word trails meanings to do with reputation: to do something to 'the *honour*' of one's nation is to do something to its 'glory', something that is worthy of its reputation, or enhances it. Thus, a person could well be said to behave 'honourably' or gloriously when behaving with courage or self-denial in a national cause, even if that cause (qv) itself were wrong.

Honour is a cousin to words like virtue, and especially to the idea of a person's having a reputation which is assumed to be virtuous, perhaps by virtue of her being a lady, of his being a gentleman (qv), and besmirching which is regarded as doing serious damage. Thus, one might defend a person's *honour* physically or verbally, especially in the Latin, Arab and Asian societies where older ideas prevail.

RICHARD D NORTH

H ONOUR (II)

Is now derided although dishonour, eg sleaze, is newsworthy.

CHARLES GOODSON-WICKES

H UNTING

In England formerly a ritualistic pastime which helped to shape the English countryside and turned vermin control into the sport of the landed class and a recreation for many followers. Now the heartless, cruel slaughter of small furry animals for pleasure by overweight, red-faced, middle-aged, upper-class gentlemen. Elsewhere *hunting* is frowned upon when it is carried out by white men of whatever age or class, but is virtuous when carried out by 'indigenous' people. When white men hunt they are despoiling nature, when 'indigenous' people hunt they are living in harmony with nature and maintaining a sustainable (qv) environment (qv).

MICHAEL MOSBACHER

HYPOCRISY

In its original usage, *hypocrisy* means deliberately and calculatedly pretending to a virtue (especially of a religious kind) that one does not possess, for the sake of reputation or gain. (See, for example, Molière's Tartuffe. Note also Rochefoucauld's maxim, that '*hypocrisy* is the tribute that vice pays to virtue', which assumes that virtue is a reality, one openly acknowledged and credited as such, and therefore worth simulating.) However, the term has come to be used to describe, and to denigrate, any virtue or moral ideal, particularly in the sexual sphere, which is particularly lofty or difficult of achievement.

The implication is that, simply because the given ideal, or indeed the ideal generally, runs counter to everyday, and persistent, human appetite, any aspiration towards it must be either deceitful or self-deceived. Even when conquered (as likely as not by 'repression'), appetite is assumed to be more 'real' or fundamental than, and thus obscurely to 'subvert', whatever endeavours to control or transcend it. Thus merely to fall short of an ideal in practice (as almost invariably happens) is to be a 'hypocrite', and to expose that ideal's worthlessness.

This presupposition, that values, virtues and ideals are simply forms of bad faith, is characteristic of the modernist, 'unmasking' tendency stemming from such thinkers as Marx, Nietzsche and Freud and still very much alive in the work of Foucault and his many disciples. Furnished with such assumptions, the most commonplace, talentless intellect fancies itself able to 'see through' the supposed 'veneer' of normal civilization to the ugly 'truth' beneath. But if anything involves pretending to a virtue (in this case perspicacity), with the aim of purchasing a reputation, the 'unmasking' habit does. It differs from traditional *hypocrisy* only in being for the most part self-deceived rather than deliberately deceitful.

ROBERT GRANT

HYPOCRITE

Formerly a *hypocrite* was someone who did not live up to his own ideals. Now hypocrisy is one of the few remaining grounds for moral opprobrium. All sorts of behaviour previously thought of as wrong or bizarre are now accepted as equally valid with the exception of one: being a *hypocrite*. If a public figure has been unmasked as a *hypocrite* everything else he might ever have said or achieved, can be dismissed with one simple sentence – 'he is a *hypocrite*'. He is then open to endless pillorying, and his career is deservedly destroyed.

MICHAEL MOSBACHER

INCLUSIVE

Form of language designed to exclude, humiliate or drive away traditionalists and conservatives from established institutions, by signalling the organizational triumph in such institutions of extreme or separatist feminism. Demonstrated by obligatory use of 'chair' instead of 'chairman' at meetings of public (qv) bodies, and refusal to accept that the word 'man' or the words 'all men' can stand for the whole human race, especially in prayers where they clearly do so.

PETER HITCHENS

INEQUALITY as in HEALTH INEQUALITY

An influential but incoherent concept spawned in the 1960s by the World Health Organization and widely deployed by those who support increased state control over the lives of ordinary people. Its classic formulation, in the Black Report of 1980 for the Department of Health and Social Security, claims that inequalities in health between social classes are grave and worsening; that their cause (qv) is poverty (qv) and unjust *inequality*; and that the only solution to the problem is massive re-distribution of wealth and income.

In fact, the health status of the whole

population has improved consistently and substantially throughout the twentieth century, as the increase in life expectancy from forty-plus to seventy-plus demonstrates. Health status differentials have also improved, with persisting excess death rates from cancer and heart disease largely attributable, not to poverty or social *inequality*, but to lifestyle decisions by individuals concerning tobacco and alcohol consumption, diet, and exercise. Increased state control and income re-distribution, as recommended in the Black Report, by subsequent commentators, and by influential elements in the Labour Party, would worsen rather than improve matters.

Despite the neglect of logic (qv) and evidence underlying the concept of *health inequality*, it is regularly – and damagingly – used in Parliament and in the media as a key component in the ritualized, incantatory defence of the outmoded principles and unreformed structures of the NHS. It serves to maintain an unreconstructed status quo in health care, and to deflect attention and resources (qv) away from real, practical problems towards political phantasies.

DAVID MARSLAND

INEVITABLE

When a radio reporter announced – regretfully it seemed – that the result of the November 1999 referendum on retaining the Australian monarchy had produced a majority in favour of retention, the reporter added, quite gratuitously, that it was *inevitable* that sooner or later Australia would dispense with the Crown. Unless one is a determinist or Marxist, however, it is perfectly obvious that nothing in politics is ever *inevitable*. If it were we would be able to predict the future; history is full of examples of history coming to a turning point and yet failing to turn. When King William V becomes a much-loved King of Australia, even the BBC might learn this truth.

ANDREW ROBERTS

INTERCOURSE

Noun. Any form of exchange between persons; now, even when lacking a qualifying adjective, taken to refer to sexual liaison.
BRYAN WILSON

INTEREST

Few have done more to give an Orwellian inversion of meaning to interest than British enthusiasts for the emerging European super-state and Britain's absorption in it. So, in recent years, we have been solemnly assured that it is in the *interest* of the world's oldest and most reliable parliamentary democracy to be, in effect, a subject province in a federation dominated by states whose democratic records and approach to government and public administration have been, should we say, questionable. We are similarly assured that it is in our *interest* to scrap our currency and embrace one that seems almost certain to fail in the long run because of the stresses and strains of the one-size-fits-all policies that underpin it. It is also in our *interest*, apparently, to toss aside centuries of sovereign law-making in exchange for laws and regulations made in Brussels. When Europhiles talk of Britain's *interest* in Europe, it is best to start counting the spoons.
DERRICK HILL

INTIMATE

Adjective. Once a cherished state of close but innocent friendship; now taken to allude usually to sexual congress.
BRYAN WILSON

INVESTMENT

As in 'Her Majesty's Government is determined to invest more in education'. Originally to 'invest' somebody was to clothe them. Hence *investment* became what was done at an investiture, the ceremonial clothing of a monarch or some lesser potentate with the robes and other accoutrements of his or her newly achieved office. Then the word began to be used to refer to the surrounding of a city by forces intending to capture it. It was only much later that people started to contrast their perhaps sometimes fecklessly improvident current spending with their prudent saving and consequent *investment* of some part of their income in hopes of a return.

So when Chancellors of the Exchequer tell us – as Chancellors have recently taken to telling us – that they are intending to invest even more of our tax money in education or whatever else they are implicitly claiming to be intending to do so in well-grounded expectations of our being rewarded by a dividend in terms of some perceived goods. So if such talk of investing is to have real substance, and not to be mere political spin, then there have to be effective methods of determining how much of the relevant perceived good actually is produced, and hence of determining whether any additional *investment* is in fact yielding an at least proportionate return.
ANTONY FLEW

JUDGEMENT

Once, good *judgement* was the criterion of a sound man. Now, like discrimination (qv), *judgement* is actively frowned upon: people are routinely (if wrongly) castigated (at least by the chattering classes) for being 'judgemental'. Being 'judgemental' is believed to be wrong, because exercising and passing judgement presupposes both the existence of meaningful standards (qv ethics), and the appropriateness of holding people responsible for achieving those standards (qv cause). Those who hold such views conveniently overlook the fact that disapproving of being judgemental itself constitutes a *judgement*.

The biblical dictum 'judge not that ye be not judged' has particular force if, as is now commonly but incorrectly supposed, there is no objective foundation for justifying or ranking *judgements* of any sort. If value and other *judgements* are no more than expressions of taste or preference, they carry little force; their truth and interest become wholly relative to the person making them. The *judgement* 'murder is wrong', made by Smith, reduces to 'Smith believes murder is wrong', or 'Smith dislikes murder', and becomes no more interesting or important than the statement 'Smith dislikes strawberry ice cream'.

Relativism about *judgements* does not only apply to the moral; it extends as well to the aesthetic and the practical. When people have little or no experience of what is good, because they have seldom if ever even been exposed to it, they may have no basis for even identifying, far less judging, what constitutes a fine picture or a good play, a well turned seam or well cooked sauce, a properly crafted chair or a sound argument.

ELAINE STERNBERG

JUST
An adverbial qualification that diminishes the seriousness of the conduct or object it qualifies. Thus '*just* a slap' means 'I broke her jaw'; '*just* burglary' means 'I am in prison because I have broken into 78 houses'; and '*just* cars' means 'I am in prison because I have stolen 219 cars and driven them away'. '*Just* heroin' or '*just* crack' are the correct answers to the question 'do you take drugs?'

THEODORE DALRYMPLE

JUSTICE
Traditionally defined as a virtue which distinguishes between good and evil, demands respect for the rights of others and punishment of wrongdoing. Now, *justice* is commonly understood to mean a UN-backed demand for the

satisfaction of a person's desires at the expense of the law and the common good. For example, the accommodation of teenage mothers is considered a right which overrules the immorality of underage sex. Again, the right to express oneself overrules the collective right not to be subjected to moral nihilism. So, in modern society pornography must be recognized as a kind of *justice*.

There are different kinds of *justice* in the modern Third Way (qv) Society, but the greatest of all is *Social* (qv) *Justice*. This is most commonly discussed on transatlantic Concorde flights to Washington, DC summits attended by expensively-clad reformed Marxists who now answer to the name of Social Democrat. Such discussions tend to plumb the complex conceptual depths involved in the idea of stealing from rich countries and using the proceeds to pay off the mortgages of the corrupt leaders of poor countries.

Social Justice also encompasses so-called 'Minority Rights'. If you feel that you belong to a Minority, then, *justice* demands that you call the Minority Hotline to find out what your minority rights are (or visit the Third Way Minority Rights Website at www.oppressed.gov.uk). Belonging to a Minority is a Good Thing. But we all know that you can have too much of a good thing. Hence, if you belong to too many minorities you may end up belonging to the Majority, which is a Bad Thing.

The problem with modern *justice* is that everyone loves to talk about it (especially on Channel 4), but no one seems to agree about what is and is not just. And that is because everyone thinks that it is a matter of opinion (hence the profound response to any moral problem – 'Who am I to judge?').

The solution to the problem of modern *justice* lies in the recognition of objective moral standards, the common good and individual responsibility. A summit on that would be nice.

DAVID S ODERBERG & ATHENA S LEOUSSI

KITCHEN

Once a room sparsely furnished in which food was prepared with skill and devotion and hard work. Now a room in which food is rarely prepared and even then with little skill, devotion or hard work. To compensate, the room is filled with expensive and largely non-active 'appliances' which are worshipped as objects in their own right.

DIGBY ANDERSON

LATE

A tendentious adjective implying that an institution, society or historical phase is coming to an end or is possibly dead already as in 'late capitalism (qv)' or 'late modernity' Probably derived by analogy from societies that really have expired as in the 'late bronze age' or the 'late medieval period'. It would be reasonable to speak of late socialism in exactly the same sense that we speak of the late President Allende or the late Leonid Brezhnev or the late Adolf Hitler, but the usage is unknown in politically-correct circles.

CHRISTIE DAVIES

LAUNCH

I am heartily sick and tired of the Prime Minister 'launching' a new 'initiative' (it is never anybody who 'launches' except the Prime Minister; cabinet ministers are left to pick up the pieces when it all goes very wrong). I would not mind so much if these 'launched' initiatives showed a single whit of genuine initiative. Habitually they are banal to a degree and after being 'launched', they promptly sink without trace.

FREDERICK FORSYTH

LEFT

An abiding term from the canon (qv) of disorder. The pursuit of socialism, of permanent unreality; the abolition of history, the world and the human condition; that is of the way things are. The old (qv) *left* sought this through abolition of the market economy, that is of society's ability to make things, through abolition of law and politics, that is of society's ability to enforce social rules according to clear, impartial standards and to adjudicate between competing claims, and through replacement of the moral canon taught by parents and churches by a new morality taught by state experts.

Following the huge contribution to freedom and affluence of the old *left* economic agenda in Russia, China, North Korea and Cuba, the new *left* now seeks socialism (egalitarianism) through non-economic means. No interest is shown in the commercial economy, except as an infinite fiscal resource (qv); but all 'right' (qv) (unequal) elements are to be identified and excised. Identifying schools and police as racist or sexist is *left* (cf showing that millions of schoolchildren are truants which is 'right'). The *left* now seeks total control of the commanding heights of education, welfare (qv) and probation by 'experts' including homosexualists, lesbians, paedophiles and other loving innovators in meaningful human relations.

The new *left* demands women priests, homosexual marriage, caring inter-specific eroticism, heroin on the National Health, capital punishment for tobacco dealers, public atonement by those accused of racism and sexism, daily apologies for British history in all newspapers and news broadcasts, removal of all advertisements which oppress and degrade women, compulsory vegetarianism, with counselling (qv) for addicted carnivores, 90 per cent female and black (qv) membership of all political bodies, equality (qv) for paraplegics in professional sport, abolition of all punishment for children, abolition of all private education, raising the school leaving age to 35, alternative (qv) lessons in all schools in all known languages, classroom instruction from years 10 and 11 in bisexual group affirmation, the immediate conversion of all FE colleges to status comparability with Oxbridge and the establishment of chairs of empowerment – reserved for ethnic (qv) minorities – in all universities (qv).

DENNIS O'KEEFFE

LEVEL PLAYING FIELD (I)

To governments, a *level playing field* is where both sides play uphill.

For example, insurance brokers promoted an Act of Parliament to regulate their profession (and squeeze out interlopers). Their distress was profound when it emerged that this new Insurance Brokers Regulation Act did not apply at all to those who did precisely the same work but called themselves 'consultants' or 'advisers' or 'intermediaries' instead of 'brokers'. So the demand went out for a *level playing field*, and before long the Financial Services Act was there to regulate each and every kind of financial service provider. Even the insurance brokers now started to complain about the cost: but at least everyone is now playing uphill.

EAMONN BUTLER

LEVEL PLAYING FIELD (II)

An appealing catchphrase often linked to that most enticing of words: 'harmonization'. Both are much favoured by Brussels protectionists to justify ceaseless imposition of higher and uniform standards on products traded in the 'single market'.

Where genuine free trade offers consumers wide choice between goods on the basis of differing qualities, performance and cost, Brussels prefers to confine choice to those goods that conform to standards acceptable to our European competitors.

Where real competition relishes the

challenging ups and downs of a golf course, Brussels 'fair trade' prefers the sedate comfort of the bowling green.

One example is the 'Social Chapter' which imposes the same hours, holidays and other 'rights' (qv) on all workers, stopping just short of a common European bedtime! To prevent 'unfair' competition from those Asian tigers, the egregious Delors once suggested a 'Global Social Charter'.

The *level playing field* is a classic example of flat earth economics.

RALPH HARRIS

M cDONALDS

Many people have not caught up with the true new meaning of this word. It might seem simply to refer to a ubiquitous chain serving up lazy and unimaginative food for which lazy and unimaginative teenagers seem to have an insatiable appetite. In fact *McDonalds* is a synonym for wickedness. To be opposed to *McDonalds* has become a test of moral worth. To hate *McDonalds* has come to be the badge of a hero. It is after all far easier to hate *McDonalds* than to do something which will actually alleviate the problems for which it is erroneously blamed. *McDonalds* has come to represent global capitalism (qv), the exploitation of the poor, the murder of animals, the destruction of rain forests, third world poverty (qv), malnutrition, and the wanton annihilation of French cultural heritage. It is ironic that *McDonalds* has done exponentially more to create a classless society than the 'anti-hierarchical' protesters who oppose it. One is as likely to find an Eton schoolboy in *McDonalds* as a boy who goes to an east London comprehensive. The rich and the poor no longer know nothing of each others' food, customs, and manners. *McDonalds* and its like every day bring together in one place what were two nations.

MICHAEL MOSBACHER

MANLINESS

Once definitive of the state or quality of vigour and virtue which differentiated a man from a woman, child or beast: chiefly, through courage, independence of mind, faith in oneself and in a cause (Tocqueville); but also by humanity, generosity and charity (Langland). Until recently, believed – and by foreigners – to be a peculiarly English quality ('the English are rather manly than warlike', Emerson). Never traditionally confined to men ('my aunt was a very manly woman', Irving); nor even to adults ('if the infant vow be invalid till the manly confirmation', Jeremy Taylor). But increasingly rendered unacceptable by a dogma which acknowledges equality only in androgyny. Consequently, a term now either unusable as approbation or appropriate (qv) only in opprobrium, indicative of mindless aggression, pointless assertiveness and/or extreme insensitivity. Femininity (amongst either men or women) is, however, widely acceptable.

SIMON GREEN

MARRIAGE

Archaic: the permanent and exclusive legal, spiritual and physical union of one man and one woman, recognized by the community, church and state. Contemporary: a relationship between two or more parties that confers on its participants the benefits (qv) of the aforementioned union with none of the responsibilities. Usage note: *marriage* has become one of those English nouns which is meaningless without an adjective, such as 'gay', 'heterosexual', 'open' (qv), 'traditional', etc.

DANIEL LAPIN

MISSION (I)

(Functional synonyms: Lava Flow, Charter) (Antonyms: Job, Task) 'This surgery (university, railway company, department store, church, betting shop, police station, etc) will provide the highest standard of service at all times'. This is a fairly typical beginning to a 'mission statement'. It has, of course, nothing to do with reality, as can be demonstrated by re-casting it as its contrary, promising to provide the worst possible service on every possible occasion. The superlatives contained in mission statements deny the relevance of the comparative: claiming to be aiming at the best becomes an excuse for not delivering the merely good-enough.

Neither is mission to be confused with its origin. Once, missions were proselytising, measurable (and often dangerous) campaigns aimed at the salvation of other people, not some generalized virtue imputed to oneself. Mission appears when some hitherto-autonomous institution is forced to justify itself to some superordinate body which has little interest in, or competence to understand the workings of the newly-subordinate body. 'Mission statements' are a form of truce or camouflage, masking the spasmodic supervisory ambitions of the former and fending-off the genuflections of the latter. They are not to be taken as generating any intensification of interest in or concern for the consumer-audience to which they are, ostensibly, addressed. People who, in appellant desperation, wave 'mission statements' in police stations, universities or surgeries are likely to be disappointed, thrown out or struck off. The very genuine victims of 'mission statements', however, are those unfortunate junior staff in the 'mission statement' issuing institution, for whom such statements exist as an ever-present proof of their own inevitable incompetence – and possible humiliation.

JON DAVIES

M ISSION (II)
The modern church is rather shy about using the word mission, at least in its original sense of an attempt to convert the heathen of

foreign lands. This partly because some foreign lands are now a good sight more Christian than the countries which converted them and partly because the church in its current mood of affirming diversity (qv) is not quite sure what to think or do about the heathen. However, the word is enjoying a renaissance in quite another sphere. The 'business community' has appropriated it. Large corporations offer to explain their *mission* to anyone who will listen. These *missions* are a bizarre lot. Monsanto is to 'create value for the world at large'; BP Amoco 'to be a force for good' in everything it does; J Sainsbury 'to contribute to the quality (qv) of life of the whole community'. These *mission* statements are full of other pseudo ethical, politically correct talk about empowerment, serving partners (qv), integrity, being a good citizen, acting responsibly and contributing to sustainability and diversity.

There is no evidence that anyone is impressed by this ethical rhetoric. Monsanto has one of the longest *mission* statements and that has not stopped it being pilloried in the media. Nor do companies need to invent *missions* for themselves since they already have a moral obligation, that of increasing return to their shareholders. Either all the missionary activity is, in fact, a means of achieving this obligation, in which case it is not in itself ethical but instrumental: or it is a diversion from the fiduciary duty to shareholders in which it might be considered unethical.
DIGBY ANDERSON

M ODERN

To be *modern* is to be 'of the present and recent times'. The idea of 'modernity' is often treated in popular parlance, as well as in art, as having a considerable moral ambiguity. Thus we refer to '*Modern* Times' or to '*modern* life' as something which may be more shallow and hectic with less time for reflective enjoyment than were their predecessors. *Modern* architecture, which rejects decoration, traditional materials and vernacular styles, has developed a particularly bad reputation. In its ambiguities modernity thus resembles 'progress'.

But despite the almost universal acceptance that change is not all good and that modernity is by no means superior to pre-modernity in all respects, governments throughout the world are able to impose projects of 'modernisation'. In doing so they are able to combine some idea of the value of modernity with the threat of its inevitability. As Lewis Silkin, Labour Minister for Town and Country Planning, said in 1946 to the inhabitants of Old Stevenage, who were protesting against the building of Stevenage New Town, 'You can shout all you like. It isn't going to make any difference.'

The better part of modernity is science and technology which are genuine improvements on their predecessors, whereas modern morals and institutions are not (necessarily) better. Good Sense can be assailed by modernity, as when the British Constitution, by far the finest working model in the world, was dismantled after 1997 by a 'New Labour' government in the interests of *modern* ideas which had, in fact, been in vogue in the 1790s. But it can also be assailed by a theory of post-modernism which claims that the idea of the *modern* is itself out-moded and which stresses that reason, science and technology are merely 'social constructs' formed to defend certain interests.

LINCOLN ALLISON

MODERN, MODERNIZING

Not simply what happens to be the case in 1999 or 2000. *Modern* is a term which implies that a certain 'modernist' agenda is being followed, even though in most cases the agenda itself is quite old. Thus *modern* art is that which derives from the now rather tired pre-1914 manifestos of Picasso and Duchamp, and cannot possibly include anything painted today according to timeless canons (qv) of beauty or representation. (Actually it is doubtful whether any painting at all would nowadays qualify as *modern*.)

In British politics *modern* is whatever fits the Project, the basic aim of which is to institute permanent government by the People's Party, government by many of the few (or something of the sort). Also called 'joined-up politics', because everyone is supposed to be included. I can't quite remember where, but I think we have heard all this before, earlier this century sometime.

ANTHONY O'HEAR

M ONETARY UNION

A top down attempt to replace local currencies and to impose one common currency on a usually large geographical area.

The demand for such unions comes from politicians who invoke economic arguments while economists mostly claim it is a political venture. Other arguments centre around either big companies which for reasons that are never clear seem unable to deal with currency risks or mythical travellers who move from country to country so rapidly that they lose all their funds in the transactions costs of constantly changing money.

The imposition of one single currency takes away the ability of local devaluations or currency movements to absorb shocks to the system. In the absence of multiple currencies one needs either free movement of labour (which exists in the US but not in the EC) or to prepare for Civil War. Even in the comparatively free USA, the inability of the South to adjust to the North's economic progress because of the lack of the South's own currency was a major cause of war.

At a time when the Governor of the Bank of England is pelted with eggs and tomatoes when he visits Scotland (because he 'sets interest rates for the south-east'), diversity in the currencies available to everybody rather than a monopoly 'union' is attracting more attention.

JOHN BLUNDELL

M YTHS

Myths are like air-cushions, there is nothing in them but they are wonderfully comforting. They represent to those who accept them a version of events which they want to believe to be true, and to which therefore they cling despite any factual evidence to the contrary. *Myths* as in, 'capitalism is a system under which the rich get richer and the poor get poorer'; poverty, as in 'undeveloped countries are caught in a vicious circle of poverty from which the developed countries have failed to rescue them'; 'the workers are never paid a 'just' wage'; etc, etc. *Myths* can be used to demonize historical figures in a way which nourishes and perpetuates grievances and allocates guilt to serve the political ends of the *myth*-makers.

BARBARA SHENFIELD

N ATIONALISM

Almost the ultimate ideological offence, usually preceded by the adjective 'narrow'. Attachment to a country and its values can only be blinkered and the enemy of the desiderata of multiculturalism and supra-*nationalism*. It leads almost inevitably to war, aggression, racialism and genocide. It apparently precludes any understanding of, and sympathy for, other nations and cultures. It suggests a self-interest on the part of the nationalists which must, by definition, disadvantage other peoples. It also requires a sense of history – which itself is often highly offensive because it evokes the achievements of people who are often white, male, aristocratic monoculturalists. It is therefore 'backward-looking' and 'divisive'. It also prevents full cooperation with other countries in such excellent enterprises as the European Union and the United Nations and is therefore arrogant. It leads to a sense of national identity which can be positively harmful – as, for example, the cohesion of the British nation and its values was so obviously dangerous in 1940, or when the desire for countries in Eastern Europe to assert their individuality proved so unnecessarily offensive to the much-lamented Soviet system.

SIMON HEFFER

N EED

Something without which you cannot be what you essentially are. Human beings *need* food and water to survive; they *need* company to become fully human, and they *need* morality to live a happy life. Apart from that they desire many things, few of which are *needs*. For example, they desire a house, a car, sexual and material success, even (though this is rarer by the day) children. These are not *needs*, but desires. By describing them as *needs*, you create a prima facie assumption that there is something wrong with a society in which people do not possess them. Hence the constant revision of socialistic accounts of what people *need* – a revision which ensures that, in any state of society conceivable, there will always be 'needy' people. In this sense the child who runs amok in the supermarket, crying 'I *need* a Mars bar', is a normal child of our time.

ROGER SCRUTON

N EGOTIATE

A word from the new moral canon (qv). The undoing of tradition, especially moral tradition. Moral tradition is a dead weight on the young. 'Negotiation' means that moral standards are not to be set by teachers and parents according to traditional rules. Instead two modern (out-comes are possible. The first is that 'negotiation' allows uncontested victory to young persons' spontaneous inclinations: children will be allowed to talk freely in class, watch as much TV and do only such homework as they fancy, eat what they want, play their music as loudly as they wish and where, and begin their active sex lives at puberty. Such negotiations will empower children and remove the oppressive rites of passage which constitute such a barrier to full child-adult equality (qv). Once children have learned successful negotiation they realize that most allegations about dangerous drugs are part of a patriarchal plot to crush the spontaneous spirit of adventure in young people. After negotiation all these adventurous experiences will be readily available. Tobacco, however, a tool of oppressive, non-negotiated American foreign policy, will be strictly forbidden.

The alternative 'negotiation' comes via teacher-facilitated 'discourse'. This will empower children through exposure to the enlightened relativism and multicultural humanism of modern teacher education. Teachers holding outmoded, oppressive, traditional views will be kept out of senior positions, to protect the children. Examinations and homework will also be 'negotiated' and in the interests of working from where the children are at, real life interests such as pop music, football and kung fu will normally have priority in academic work. Elitist, racist and sexist culture (qv), as in Shakespeare and Mozart, will normally be excluded under negotiation. The emphasis at all times will be on children negotiating their own knowledge. Negotiating means that everyone will construct her own reality (qv), and history will for the first time include her story.

Under teacher-facilitated negotiation too, children will be free to do as they wish, and they will also learn how wicked it is to be male or white or British or heterosexual or affluent or human. They will be empowered to hate

tobacco, and endorse homosexuality, by learning to recognize how gay it is.
DENNIS O'KEEFFE

O BSCENE

For centuries it usefully went about its business denoting acts or words that are repulsively or offensively indecent. Then came the 1960s, when those of a liberal outlook proclaimed it a word with no apparent practical application. According to a travelling circus of literary and cultural 'experts' called to give evidence in a series of prosecutions brought under the Obscene Publications Act of 1959 – notably the prosecution of Penguin Books, publishers of D H Lawrence's Lady Chatterley's Lover – it was impossible to define what was *obscene*. One man's bestiality is another's beauty was the thrust of their argument. Besides, works of literary merit should not be subject to the normal rules of decency.

But just as *obscene* seemed to have been condemned to the lexicographical dustbin, left-liberal opinion suddenly spotted legitimate applications for it. Thus, any economic or social (qv) outcome of which leftists and liberals disapprove is denounced as *obscene*. Large profits are often anathematized as *obscene*, likewise the salaries and perks of company executives, and the activities of multinationals, particularly as they have an impact on the environment (qv). Military action is often *obscene*, though mostly when conducted in defence of Western interests. Inequality, in general, but especially when relating to race or gender, is also thought suitable for the epithet which, in its traditional contexts, dare not speak its name. Indeed, it has become an all-purpose boo-word for anything of which one disapproves strongly – always provided, of course, that the anything in question is not just repulsively or offensively indecent.
DERRICK HILL

OLD

As in 'good *old* so-and-so' or 'fine *old* wine' used to be a term of affection or endearment. Likewise as applied to people, *old* used to imply wisdom, experience, measured judgement as against the wildness and impetuosity of youth.

Now the cult of youth and modernity has changed all that. The term is used pejoratively as in '*Old* Labour' in contrast with more desirable 'New Labour'. New World, New Age, *vin nouveau* even, these are the hype things. At your peril do you promote in today's world what is *old*, what has stood the test of time, what is mature, what is well known and tested.

However, there is a big problem for this new way of thinking – *old* people. You cannot, by the new standards, talk pejoratively about people because of what they are. Such would be the height of political incorrectness. There is no escaping that *old* people do become an inconvenience in today's new, vibrant, youthful culture. What to do? There seem to be four responses. First, is to treat *old* people as yet another threatened minority, like gays, the disabled or blacks (qv). This way young people can take up the cudgels 'on their behalf' in the struggle against 'ageism' and campaign for more resources (qv) for the chronologically challenged. The second response is to pretend that ageing in the human being simply does not happen – the 'you're as *old* as you feel' syndrome. This leads to many absurdities such as plastic surgery, fitness work-outs for the over sixties, daft diets, unproven food complements, herbs, vitamins, and so on, to maintain the pretence that time and the great reaper are not taking effect. Then there are 'homes' where the olds can be packed away safely invisible. And the final solution increasingly favoured now – euthanasia.

JOHN GREENWOOD

OPEN

Used almost invariably in a positive sense. Nations should be open, families should be *open*, clubs and associations should be *open*, schools should be *open*. The state is put in charge of ensuring that everything is *open*, and non-discriminatory. But can any form of social life exist without discrimination (qv)? Hardly so. The fabric of any kind of society is represented by the freedom of people to agree to co-operate with others of their choice. Choosing is just another name for discrimination. We discriminate when we marry, have a party, found a company. Why should people be forced to accept into their societies those that they do not like? And why should one have the right to acceptance by others? Beyond the unconditioned praise for 'openness' we find the twin concepts that material equality (qv) is more important than individual freedom, and that traditions and customs are essentially bad, and should therefore be more or less eliminated.

ANGELO M PETRONI

OPPORTUNITY

An event or moment that presents itself to all living persons every day of their lives. An *opportunity* lies dormant, however, unless first recognized as an *opportunity* and then seized upon. This process is sometimes called 'making one's *opportunity*'. Because *opportunities* are often difficult to identify as *opportunities*, many are missed, or sometimes called 'lost'. *Opportunities* abound in free markets that reward the risk-taking necessary to capitalize on an *opportunity*. *Opportunities* can be stifled and even denied to large portions of a society, such as those that suffer from excessive government regulation and state control of markets, as occurred in Soviet Russia. Those few who find *opportunities* in such a stifling environment are called 'opportunists'.

GRAEME NEWMAN

ORDER as in OUT OF ORDER

'Order' is both a form of controlled behaviour and the system of rules by which it is regulated. Actions may be *out of order* in both senses: behaviour may be uncontrolled or it may deviate from established norms. The contexts of orderly behaviour are diverse. The Speaker of the House of Commons announces the start of business with the words 'Order, order' and the master of ceremonies at a darts tournament asks for 'The very best of order please'. In neither of these cases, of course, is the appeal without a significant measure of wishful thinking.

Order in these senses operates by consensus or by the collective acceptance of received rules. The norms of order are fixed and predetermined.

What distinguishes order in the modern sense is the principle of personal whim. Order is not a system but an attitude of intolerance centred on the self. When a person describes an action as *out of order* or – more probably – 'totally *out of order*', we discover the extent to which that person has not been able to allow or accommodate the needs (qv) and interests (qv) of other beings. Those not vested with formal authority to govern a social situation take on the attitude of a jury.

The scholarly study of moral development has tended to identify an egocentric stage in infancy and an altruistic stage as human beings mature and recognize the needs of a world apart from themselves. The concept of order has naturally belonged to the altruistic stage but it now operates within an egocentric world view.

In its latest usage, *out of order* reflects a fundamental change in the application of a moral view. Formerly order was a discipline imposed upon the individual. Now order is an adjustment, which the individual requires of the world.

ROGER HOMAN

ORGANIC

The taxonomy of a big supermarket, clearly the result of intense thought and 'creative' imagination, is a fascinating study. To begin with, in a clear reference to the Garden of Eden, fruit and vegetables are always placed next to the entrance, inducing soothing green (qv) thoughts and a relaxed disposition to buy. During the last few years an even more seductive subsection has appeared: 'Organic Produce'.

The word *organic* has acquired immense, indeed magical power. It carries associations of purity; of the natural order as against polluted, man-made industrial horror; of the Wordsworthian healing power of Nature herself; even of happy, sunburned peasants labouring in the fields of Old England, where agro-technical machines and chemical pesticides with sinister-sounding names were as yet unknown.

That genuine *organic* produce is good for you can hardly be doubted. Nor can the eagerness of unscrupulous producers to exploit the sheer power of the word in the market, which induces the gullible to pay more for goods they believe to be *organic*, often on no more evidence than the label. Eggs may be labelled *organic* merely because they do not, it is claimed, come from battery fowls. There is 'organic tea' and 'organic chewing gum'. Could a sales campaign for 'organic cigarettes' prevail even over another kind of health fanaticism?

MICHAEL WHARTON

OUTING

Formerly an innocent activity, such as an excursion or picnic for inner city children in the clean air and green acres of the countryside followed by a romp (qv) over the hills. Now the blackmailing, for political ends, of public (qv) figures – especially politicians, bishops, and generals – by activists promoting their own conception of the rights (qv) of homosexuals. The public figures' alleged 'offence' is to be closeted, ie, not wanting to discuss private matters publicly. It is important to note that if a tabloid newspaper alleges that a public figure is homosexual this is homophobic; if self-appointed, self-selected spokesmen for the so-called gay community (qv) do the exact same thing they are 'striking a blow against homophobia' (qv).

MICHAEL MOSBACHER

OVERARCHING AUTHORITY THE NEED FOR A

A phrase used whenever somebody wants an issue centralized so that a big budgeted government agency can be put in charge of it, and the speaker put in charge of the agency.

MATT RIDLEY

PARTNER

Originally meaning a business *partner* or a professional colleague, eg 'My partner Dr Smith'. The word indicated an extreme and reassuring respectability coupled with a formal distance (qv). For instance, *partners* often used to work together for a quarter of a century without using Christian names.

But when marriage (qv) fell into disfavour in the 1980s, a word had to·be found that avoided the embarrassment of having to introduce one's cohabitee. Few liberals had the nerve to introduce their lover as, 'My mistress Miss Smith'. *Partner* came into favour. The word, with its air of Victorian solidity brought an air of permanence and rectitude to what was often no more than simple fornication.

Conversely, it allowed the frightened liberal to conceal the shameful respectability of being married from his liberal friends. 'This is my *partner* Mary' can mean anything from casual cohabitation in a free love commune to 40 years of Church of England married rectitude.

Partner came fully into its own with the rise of legalized homosexuality in the 1970s. A male introducing another male as his partner at a party is almost certainly a practising 'gay'.

Yet the original meaning of the term still lingers. This can present difficulties for students of good manners. A doctor might talk about 'My *partner* Dr X' only to suffer severe embarrassment when he sees a look of liberal complicity spreading on the faces of his listeners. An attempt to remedy this by saying he meant 'Dr X was his medical *partner* rather than his `gay' companion', risks the admission that he disapproves of 'gays'. To those with robust views this may not seem much of a risk, but people these days are easily embarrassed. A better word, for both heterosexual and homosexual relationships would be 'my lover'. It is clear, honest, and at least the speaker has the courage of his convictions. Otherwise one is left with the American alternative, 'significant other'. This term, with its queasy admission of half-hearted, conditional emotional attachment, is so repellent as to be barely repeatable. *Partner* is, however, unlikely to be used for necrophiliac relationships as introductions to friends are seldom necessary if you consort with the dead.

MYLES HARRIS

P ATRIARCHY

Properly a technical word, referring to the dignity, see or jurisdiction of an ecclesiastical patriarch; more broadly, the definition of a system of government of a family, tribe or community by the father or eldest male (ie by one man, not by all men). Rendered meaningless by feminist social theory which sees it as an 'important term used in a variety of ways to characterize abstractly the structures and social arrangements within which women's oppression is elaborated' (Sheila Rowbotham). This oppression of every woman by every man now affects women 'everywhere, even in outer space and the future' (Mary Daly). Nor are the effects of

such universal 'colonization' limited to the regions 'outside women's minds'; rather, they are 'internalized, festering inside women's heads, even feminists' heads' (idem). Comment is superfluous.
SIMON GREEN

PATRIOTISM (I)

(Archaic) One who defends his country's freedom (from patris, fatherland in Greek). The British people in the past used this word to indicate a love of their own country while inferring no dislike for any other. This meaning has been corrected by decrees that any inhabitant of Britain satisfied with any characteristic of his country must be wilfully ignorant of the superiority of all other countries. This being clearly racist, the use of the word should no longer be allowed, pending the necessary legislation. In the meantime, permission is granted for progressive writers to use the word in a pejorative sense, eg 'the English football thugs showing their *patriotism* by storming down the streets of Paris in their usual state of drunken debauchery'.
RICHARD BODY

PATRIOTISM (II)

The opposite of cosmopolitanism and its offspring, globalism, with both of which it tends to be unfavourably compared. *Patriotism* is a sentiment of attachment to a particular territory and a particular cultural community which inhabits this territory and determines its laws, ie the shape which life takes within this clearly delimited space. The term *patriotism* describes a person's attachment to what the ancients called patria and we now call the nation-state. *Patriotism* expresses the human need for rootedness and differentiation. It expresses the human need for community, for deep, personal relations which can only flourish within stable and hence territorially circumscribed population groups.

The objects of *patriotism*, the particular group and land which one cherishes and wishes to protect, may be given at birth or chosen by naturalisation.

Patriotism is a necessary component of membership in all free societies, ancient or modern (qv). In these societies membership is not, or not necessarily, ascriptive (eg derived from birth) but once granted, it acquires the emotional features of family membership and of homecoming. Naturalisation is like an adoption and should be revered as such. Liberal-democratic societies are societies whose political life is shaped by shared ideas, values and decisions, and is thereby national. This feature of free societies binds its members into a community of citizens, a community of destiny, interdependence and responsibility. Free societies as open, non-authoritarian societies, depend for their cohesion, more than any other form of society, on the *patriotism* of their members, their love of country. And this love, this personal commitment to maintain the polity despite the occasional losses, depends on the freedom to participate in the constitution of the national life.

Liberal-democratic societies are communities of participation – moral and political. Human Rights legislation regarding citizenship tends to overlook this fact. First, the 'human right' to free movement and citizenship of all men and women everywhere tends to transform free, settled and prosperous political communities into places of temporary and free accommodation, into 'not here, there'. Second, for these modern legislators, citizenship should not require any degree of assimilation, or moral commitment to the values of the host community, let alone the highest commitment, to stay and die, albeit sweetly, for one's (adopted) homeland, 'pro patria mori'. These principles of non-participation and arbitrary exit have destabilising effects on the host community. They disrupt the normal flow of civil and political exchanges and, at the point of exit, incur debts – both material and psychological.

Human beings are, by nature, patriotic, which is another word for not only sociable but also loyal in sociability. Some philosophers of history and of the new millennium dismiss such human impulses and affections as belonging to the past, to primitive and transient stages of the human heart, and present us with the evolved, global man. The new, global man has no fatherland but has his own TV and radio shows, and has replaced, in social (qv) science and political folklore, the Soviet man to whom, however, he bears a striking resemblance.

ATHENA S LEOUSSI

P EACE

1. Surrender, usually to inferior and morally repulsive forces, justified purely by the absence of open conflict which results, as in 'Peace Process' in Northern Ireland and the Middle East. Unpublicized and surreptitious conflict may continue, provided it is carried out unofficially or by 'dissidents', and preferably with bludgeons and iron bars rather than with guns and explosives.

2. Disarmament at moment of national danger, while the enemy remains fully armed, as in 'Greenham Common Peace Women' (eccentrics who believed the Soviet Union should be the only nuclear power in Europe) or 'Peace March' (a procession of KGB dupes).

3. Appeasement of superior force, accompanied by delusions of good faith, as in 'Peace with Honour' (territorial surrender with disastrous strategic implications, given in return for unenforceable promise of non-aggression) and 'Peace in Our Time' (war next year).

4. (In Middle East only) 'Land for Peace' (See 'Peace with Honour').

PETER HITCHENS

PERVERTED

A desire is *perverted* if it diverges from what is normal or natural. Since bien pensant opinion denies that there is such a thing as normal or natural sexual desire – children have long ago been removed from the equation – it is no longer politically correct to talk of sexual perversion, but only of 'alternative (qv) sexualities'. Perversion now means behaving like a 'savage', ie, like a natural example of homo sapiens. In current terms this means that those who hunt, eat meat or wear fur coats, or those who punish children in the traditional way, are likely to be regarded as perverts. In the PC understanding of the term, a pervert is probably faithfully married, hardworking, and devoted to his children, with an active interest in gardening, church and field sports. His perversion is revealed in such traits as homophobia (qv), a respect for discipline, and the habit of being 'judgemental' when it comes to the question of sex.

ROGER SCRUTON

POST

A piece of wood used to stake out the purported terminating boundary of flourishing institutions, as in 'post-industrial society', 'post-modern', 'post-Christian', 'post-capitalist'. However, unsurprisingly, given the accelerating spread and penetration of bureaucracy at the present time, no-one has yet invented the 'post-office society'.

CHRISTIE DAVIES

POVERTY

(Functional synonyms: Third World, Big Issue, Jobless) (Functional antonyms: Donald Trump, Enough) There is money in *poverty*. To the relief of hundreds of sociologists, social (qv) workers, epidemiologists and socialists, the Poor are always with us. How can this be?

'The poor – all who have been and are being disabled by social, economic, cultural, religious or emotional deprivation, and are hungry for change': this is a fairly typical contemporary 'definition' of *poverty*. The fact that this 'definition' is almost total, if amiable nonsense, does not matter. It is meant to define not so much an objective situation as an exhortatory and virtuous attitude. To retain the word *poverty* to highlight the misery (sic) of what must, by such definitions, be countless numbers of people, is to retain an image of society as morally divided into The Poor and their enemy The Rich. The fact that most of us (being credit-worthy members of the middle class) are neither poor nor rich, is elided and the great game of rich versus poor retained in all its apocalyptic, and totally idiotic drama.

A recent extension of *poverty* is 'socially excluded', a term imputing agency to someone (the rich?) deliberately setting out to make people 'poor'. Both definitions, especially when conflated, create even vaster numbers of people who are 'poor' either through no fault of their own or because of a conspiracy. Of course, by far the greater number of 'The Poor' deeply resent both such a designation and the endless representations of their own irrelevance to their own lives. Most 'poor' people do not believe and would not recognize what is said about them. Our 'poor' exist primarily to give balm to the nostalgic, disaffected and uneasy worries of newly-comfortable 'professionals', socially included in that cheerful vested interest called the 'Poverty Lobby'.

JON DAVIES

P RACTICE as in BEST PRACTICE

Commonly used in large state-controlled entities such as the National Health Service, local authority social (qv) service departments, and the comprehensive school system. Highest common factor in a system where equality (qv) is more important than excellence (qv). A poor-to-mediocre standard of achievement which meets

the moral targets of modern liberal orthodoxy, can be attained without attracting charges of elitism (qv), and which can be defended against the complaints of all those too poor to afford an alternative, if one exists.
PETER HITCHENS

P RECAUTIONARY PRINCIPLE (I)

An excuse for blocking any change, even change for the better on the grounds, 'better safe than sorry'. By maximising potential unknown dangers and ignoring potential unknown benefits, those who embrace 'precaution' argue against all technological and economic progress. The *precautionary principle* would have prevented the invention of vaccines, antibiotics, railways, computers and hybrid maize – all of which had unknown hazards attached.
MATT RIDLEY

P RECAUTIONARY PRINCIPLE (II)

The notion that new products, methods and innovations should not be permitted by the state if there is the slightest risk, however remote and in however a small number of cases, that they might eventually cause harm. The principle demands that the benefits of the new product, however clear, immediate and widespread should be ignored.

The *precautionary principle* however only applies to innovation by corporations and other traditional 'enemies of the people' such as farmers. Various environmentalist web sites are instructive as to the correct usage of this concept. Such sites argue that GM crops should not be permitted because it is uncertain as to whether long-term risks may not be associated with them. They argue that however small the likelihood of these dangers, it is not a risk worth taking. Some of these sites go on to discuss the drug, Ecstasy. They correctly state that, in an albeit very small number of cases, Ecstasy use has led to sudden death and that some broader concerns have been raised about the possible long-term consequences upon the brain of heavy, regular Ecstasy use. One might think such sites, invoking their favoured *precautionary principle*, would support current restrictions on Ecstasy. However such sites advise people to be aware of the risks, take precautions and make up their own minds as to whether to use ecstasy. So the *precautionary principle* applies to GM foods (should be banned – too dangerous to let the consumer decide), but not to Ecstasy (make up your own minds). The sites point out that the incidences of death through Ecstasy use are aberrant, but never make the same point when they highlight the deleterious consequences some individuals have suffered from a corporate product. This tells us more about the prejudices of some environmentalists than anything else. Gangsters are obviously more to be trusted than corporations. The fact that corporations are liable to be sued if their products have deleterious consequences, and drug dealers – because their products are illegal – are immune from such consequences, is irrelevant. One may come to the conclusion that the invocation of the *precautionary principle* is really about opposition to the corporation, not about safety itself.

MICHAEL MOSBACHER

PREVENTION

The most potent term in the lexicon of the New Public Health (qv). The source of its popularity is as follows. *Prevention* is better than cure for precisely the same self-evident reason as 'a stitch in time saves nine'. Indeed, with diseases such as cancer, much of the time 'cure' is not even an option so *prevention* is not just 'better' but incomparably superior. The main requirement in preventing a disease is to know its cause, which is straightforward enough with lung cancer and strokes which are caused by smoking and raised blood pressure respectively. But these only account for a small minority – 10 per cent – of all deaths. So clearly, if the remaining 90 per cent are to be prevented, the responsible agents must be identified. This is easily done. Take one group of people with a particular disease, another without and compare their everyday lives – what they eat and drink, their sexual habits and leisure activities. Any differences that are identified are then labelled as a 'risk factor' which, if avoided, will result in the disease being 'prevented'.

This 'preventive' approach to disease has proved infinitely fertile, keeping the new public health practitioners gainfully employed identifying one new and unexpected threat to health after another. The only drawback is that the scientific evidence is either marginal or contradictory – alcohol has and has not been linked with cancer of the breast; coffee has or has not been linked with cancer of the pancreas; and the same applies to yoghurt and cancer of the ovary, vaginal douching and cancer of the cervix, regular mouthwashes with cancer of the mouth and eating red meat with cancer of the colon, and so on ad virtually infinitum.

This contradictory evidence can, however, be readily accommodated within the precautionary principle (qv) – if it's not possible to be absolutely sure about the latest 'risk factor', it is only sensible to presume it must be true and act accordingly. When it comes to *prevention*, it would seem, you just cannot have too much of it.
JAMES LE FANU

P RICE CONTROL
An attempt by government to control the laws of supply and demand, *price controls* are usually accompanied by income controls. Issued at times of high price increases, such controls usually occur 12 to 18 months after the currency has been inflated. No known example of a

successful attempt to control prices and incomes can be found. Even in Babylonian times when prices were carved in stone (dolomite actually) or Roman times when the death penalty was invoked by Diocletian, *price controls* failed. Attempts in the US and UK in the early 1970s under Nixon and Heath led employers to come up with many ingenious ways of avoidance. Today, with general acceptance of the Friedman position that inflation is always and everywhere a monetary phenomenon, such controls are widely discredited. However, this does not stop governments from trying to intervene in specific markets such as football club tickets and shirts.

JOHN BLUNDELL

PROFIT

Even supposedly modernized socialist parties still maintain that primitive antipathy to *profit* and to inequalities (qv) associated with it, which derives from their anti-capitalist ideological roots. Indeed, the schools, the universities, and the media are continually extending the enervating grip of this destructively sentimental prejudice far beyond the ranks of politically-committed socialists.

Yet, along with patriotism (qv) and love of family, the *profit* motive is the major driving force in the dynamics of any free society. A capitalist economy where vision, innovation, determination, effort and enterprise are rewarded by *profit* is essential in any successful, stable democracy. Suppress the *profit* motive, and national bankruptcy, shortly followed by the subversion of freedom, is inevitable. Expressions of 'anger at Railtrack's £1.3m a day *profits*' (to quote a tabloid headline), and earlier condemnation of the 'excessive *profits*' of successful privatized utilities and the 'fat-cat salaries' of their 'shamelessly greedy' directors demonstrate just how dangerously influential the politics of envy remains in Britain.

Despite the challenges to socialist bureau-cracy and the hand-out culture preferred so courageously by Margaret Thatcher, the British people apparently prefer loss to *profit*, the cocoon of state welfare to self-reliance in a com-petitive market, and the poverty of equality to profit-driven progress all round. My home ency-clopedia absurdly has an entry for 'profit-shar-ing' – and none for *profit*! The Pocket Oxford Dictionary does at least manage to include *profit*, but defines it as 'pecuniary gain, excess of returns over outlay', and exemplifies it with 'the *profits* are enormous'.

DAVID MARSLAND

P ROMISCUOUS

Adjective. Mixed, indiscriminate; now used almost solely of random and rampant sexual proclivity.

BRYAN WILSON

P UBLIC

The *public* world is traditionally understood to concern activities outside the immediate sphere of an individual person or family group. *Public* companies are those where ownership is not confined to a restricted circle. *Public* educa-tion is education provided to many pupils from diverse families, in contrast to education provid-ed by private tutors to a particular pupil or group of pupils within the family. With the growth of the state, the word *public* began to apply to any activity undertaken by the govern-ment or its agents. A *public* service became any service supplied by the government rather than any service used by members of the *public*.

The association of *public* services with supply by the state led to further possibilities for confusion. *Public* is now frequently used as an adjective implying that a good or service should be supplied 'free of charge'. Thus the '*public* highway' is not simply a highway used by 'the *public*' in contrast to a private drive or lane, it is a highway without a toll. If higher education or health are referred to as '*public* services', the speaker usually intends to convey a message that they should be supplied free of charge by the state.

MARTIN RICKETTS

PUBLIC HEALTH

A nineteenth-century term to describe those aspects of hygiene concerned with protecting the populace against the hazards of infectious illnesses such as cholera. Its great exponent was Edwin Chadwick – author of 'A report on the sanitary conditions of the labouring population of Great Britain' (1842) – who recommended implementation of what he called 'the sanitary idea' directing local boards of health to provide drainage, paving, drinkable water, together with the regulation of 'dwellings, nuisances and offensive drains'.

Chadwick's initiation of a massive civil engineering programme involved the construction of new drainage and sewage removal systems. Though opposed by conservatives ('a little dirt and freedom may after all be more desirable than no dirt at all and slavery') it had a profound effect on controlling the spread of contagious epidemics and in increasing life expectancy.

In the late twentieth century, the legacy of Chadwick's estimable reforming zeal was revived in the form of the *New Public Health*. Here the cause of modern illnesses (such as heart disease and cancer), it was argued, lay simply in people's 'unhealthy lifestyle' – insufficient exercise, eating the wrong sorts of food, and excessive tobacco consumption.

They could similarly be controlled but not this time by 'civil', but rather by 'social' engineering. This has entailed bamboozling the public into believing their illnesses are primarily their own fault and cajoling them into making substantial changes to their everyday lives. The main difference, however, between the 'old' and 'new' *public health* is that the former was based on science and worked, while the latter is not and does not.

JAMES LE FANU

Q UALITY

As in '*quality* assurance', '*quality* control'. A device for diverting 'resources' (qv) away from producers and into ever-expanding bureaucracy; in contemporary parlance, *quality* signifies the imposition of crass managerialism on an organization which may have been perfectly efficient to start with, precisely because it was lightly administered; but it certainly will not be afterwards, as in our universities, and the National Health Service. In institutional mission (qv) statements, the word *quality* can normally be substituted by the word 'mediocrity' without loss of sense or truth or value.

ANTHONY O'HEAR

R EALITY

T S Eliot once famously said that most people cannot bear too much *reality*. This may be true in the modern (qv) world of airport novels and Harrison Ford movies. However, it may be surprising to learn that people once were quite serious about *reality* – they even believed in its existence. They accepted that there was such a thing as the world out there.

Now, for the Man of Late Modernity, the world out there has been transformed into the world in here – the world six feet in front of the sofa. This world is a small black box and it contains all of modern *reality*: suffering, love, heartbreak, joy, the Amazonian rainforest, the National Lottery, the new VW G Series, Michael Ignatieff and new soft Andrex. What more could we ask for at the dawn of the new Millennium?

The problem with so-called 'Late Modernity'

is that you might see Neighbours on television, but you'll be lucky if you see neighbours on the street. The *reality* of the community has been replaced by the 'virtual *reality*' of Eastenders. These people owe you nothing and all you owe them is a blank stare every evening. In fact, the *reality* of family life itself is being replaced by the cartoon reality of The Simpsons. The new species of man, the four-fingered Homo Simpsonius, seems to be the ideal role model for the modern Cyber Child. For even though Homer Simpson does not take care of his children, fails to discipline them and positively encourages their delinquency, all of this is redeemed by the One Great Virtue: they all watch TV together. Every night.

DAVID S ODERBERG & ATHENA S LEOUSSI

R **ECLAIM** as in 'RECLAIM THE STREETS'
Formerly meant the taking back of some-thing by those who possessed it as of right. *Reclaim* has, however, acquired a rather different new meaning through the somewhat unusual slogan '*reclaim the streets*' or '*reclaim our streets*'. This slogan has come into the public eye due to various imaginative protests in the UK – similar, albeit on a smaller scale, to those against the World Trade Organization in Seattle and other cities – based around it: the so-called 'Carnivals against Capitalism' and various 'Guerrilla Gardening' events. These spectacles claim to *reclaim* – by slouching, singing, sloga-neering and smashing up a capitalist enterprise here and defacing the occasional war memorial there – public space for 'ordinary' people. This is said to let 'ordinary' people use and enjoy public space as it was intended by allowing them to interact voluntarily and peacefully with each other for their mutual benefit. *Reclaiming* is supposedly a temporary liberation from the shackles of capitalism, with the hope that it will give people the confidence and self-belief – the

empowerment – to permanently overthrow the system. Any violence which occurs while public space is being 'reclaimed', it is argued, is as nothing to the violence heaped daily on the planet by capitalism.

This use of *reclaim* is rather unusual in that these public spaces have already been claimed, for their mutual benefit, by many millions of 'ordinary people'. These millions are every day claiming public space by using and enjoying it, interacting voluntarily and peacefully with each other. They are the millions of 'ordinary' people who choose to shop in their local grocers, newsagents, and butchers, in Sainsburys, Tescos, and W H Smith – organizations which on a daily basis supply reliable, safe, quality goods at reasonable prices, doing more to empower 'ordinary people' in a single day than would be achieved by a thousand years of demonstrations.

What the protesters claim they want is already happening. Except far from a rejection of consumer capitalism being the way of achieving this aim, consumer capitalism has been the conduit for it.

The millions who daily peacefully claim the streets contrast with the – at the very highest estimates – 10,000 who, with a myriad of divergent objectives only united by a hatred of capitalism, every six months or so *'reclaim the streets'*. The millions are using public space as it has always been used. The development of public space, indeed its very existence, is intertwined with the development of commerce. How the demonstrators can claim to be *'reclaiming'* public space by stopping commerce is a baffling use of the word.

'Reclaim the Streets' calls itself a 'disorganization' – a term meaning that they have no formal leaders, have no fixed membership, and anyone can claim to act autonomously in their name. (This is an organizational structure which they claim exemplifies the kind of society they

are trying to build, but it has unhappy antecedents. It was first adopted in recent times by neo-nazi racist terror gangs who called it 'leaderless resistance', and then adopted by the Animal Liberation Front). 'Reclaim the Streets' is the modernized, new face of protest. Although its objectives are very different from New Labour, these protesters represent the Blairification of protest. They both mark the triumph of style over substance. What is immediately noticeable about 'Reclaim the Streets' is not what they are campaigning for, but the innovative and lively nature of the spectacles they produce, or rather 'disorganize'. What matters is not what the protesters demand, but what the protest looks like. This is protest as spectacle, protest as entertainment, protest as a style statement. It is revolution for the fun of it.

MICHAEL MOSBACHER

REFUTE

Frequently used by speakers who mean only that an opponent's words have been gainsaid. The correct word here is repudiate. By contrast, a 'refutation' is a collected series of statements which actually disproves or otherwise totally invalidates a proposition. 'I *refute* that!' exclaims the government minister with all the arrogance of ignorance. All he really *refutes* here, and that unconsciously, is the unspoken proposition that he has any sense of vocabulary.

PETER MULLEN

RESOURCES

The Concise Oxford Dictionary defines *resources* as a means of supplying a want. *Resource* has not so much changed its meaning as had it narrowed and seized by one particular interest. When family breakup or unemployment or poor schooling are declared to be the result of 'lack of *resources*' this does not mean *resources* of character, morality, enterprise or even knowledge. It means not enough government hand-outs and hence inadequate levels of taxation. It is odd that those who condemn modern commercial culture for being materialistic have themselves corrupted the word *resource* into mere money and other people's at that.

DIGBY ANDERSON

R ESPECTABLE

An ancient term of approval. Indicative of qualities worthy of respect; amongst human beings primarily by reason of their moral excellence. Interpreted by the Victorians as the appropriate recognition of honesty or decency in character, invariably without reference to social position. Hence Harriet Martineau: 'All labour for which there is a fair demand is equally *respectable*'. Denigrated by their successors as the archetypal vehicle of elitism (qv), hypocrisy (qv) and repressiveness. Thus the notable priapist, Eric Gill, 'With all the snobs and sycophants and, above all, the *respectable* there is nothing to be done'. Now universally associated with all such vices, seemingly most common amongst constitutionally uncommunicative post-adolescents. In the authoritative words of the Guardian: 'Middle-aged *respectables* tend to shy away from discussion'.

SIMON GREEN

R IGHT as in RIGHT WING

The idea that politics could be seen as a contest between the *right* and the 'left' (qv) originated in the recalled French States General of 1789 when the commoners sat on the King's left and the aristocracy on his *right*. It is an idea which persisted in subsequent National Assemblies and, indeed, spread to the whole world. The 'left wing' in politics have always been identified with reform and redistribution, the '*right* wing' with defence of some conception of the status quo.

It is indicative that the Oxford Dictionary of Politics offers a definition of 'left' but none of *right*. For most of the twentieth century, 'the left' often had a relatively clear meaning within the context of particular national politics: to be 'left' was to favour social equality, public ownership and the redistribution of wealth. But a person might oppose the left from a range of different points of view: one could be a clerical monarchist, a fascist (qv), an authoritarian racist, a libertarian, or a utilitarian economist who believed in free markets and still be perceived as 'on the *right*'. In effect, *right* just meant 'not-left' and to talk as if there were really a *right*-wing position per se in politics was just a simple kind of mistake, like thinking that Canterbury and Oxford are really the same place because they are the same distance from London. Some people on the left clearly did believe that (say) Louis XIV, Genghis Khan, Adolf Hitler and Margaret Thatcher were in some sense really the same. Thus the sort of moral indignation which could be summoned against Hitler could be redirected against Thatcher.

In the late twentieth century, it became more obviously incoherent to talk about the *right* because, with the collapse of socialist projects all over the world, it was much less easy to identify the left. Was it more left-wing to be a believer in direct democracy, a proponent of minority rights, a 'green' (qv) who sought to change man's relations with nature, or a remaining believer in a modicum of public ownership? Even being 'not-left' had lost much of its meaning.
LINCOLN ALLISON

RIGHTS

Undoubtedly, the most inflated political and moral category of contemporary political language. In good old times, *rights* were considered as a property of individuals. Individuals were conceived to have *rights* on their own person, as well as on the property that they had legitimately acquired. The *rights* owned by each individual corresponded to the duty of respecting the *rights* of others. Everything has changed with the rise of the socialist view of man and society. *Rights* no longer bear any connection to property. People are assumed to have *rights* independently from the way they did, or from their moral worth. They have a *right* to a 'decent' income, to 'adequate' medical care, even to 'good consideration' by other people. *Rights* are no longer a matter of individuals, but are a 'social' (qv) matter. Thus, the so-called 'social *rights*' have overcome the individual's *rights*. On behalf of society, individuals can have their *rights* limited, even cancelled. They cannot choose the education they prefer for themselves and their children. Choice in health care is also severely limited. Their income is progressively taxed in order to ensure that governments can provide 'social services'. Proliferation of *rights* is conducive to a childish society. Everybody feels that if things are not going the way they like, the fault is due to the 'society' that has not given them their fair share of *rights*. The sense of individual responsibility in cases of distress, old age, or for one's family, is giving way to the worst moral vices: envy and resentment.

ANGELO M PETRONI

R OMP
Formerly a brisk, bracing, wholesome walk through the countryside. Now a sordid sexual escapade in a seedy hotel involving a celebrity and at least two other persons – three if you include the journalist.

MICHAEL MOSBACHER

S CRUPULOUSNESS
A failing characteristic of those limited minds who believe that the invigorating generalizations with which our modern age is so

plentifully stocked may need occasionally to be checked against individual facts.
DAVID WOMERSLEY

SELF-ESTEEM

When it was first developed in the post-war years as one item in the extensive armoury of tools with which personality and behaviour were analyzed, the concept of *self-esteem* was useful to a degree, and certainly did little harm. Since then, however, it has elbowed aside other dimensions of personality, including neuroticism, extroversion, anxiety, span of attention and, especially, intelligence. To measure the latter is nowadays regarded as politically incorrect if not actually sinful.

Social scientists specializing in education have taken the lead in shifting *self-esteem* first to centre-stage and, latterly, to a monopoly position in the analysis of children's behaviour. Teachers are seriously encouraged in the universities (qv), where they are trained, to believe that only lack of positive *self-esteem* prevents their pupils from succeeding. Differences in capacity and character, which objectively matter rather more, are unthinkingly dismissed and ignored. As the counselling (qv) industry has inexorably expanded, programmes designed to increase *self-esteem* have sprung up like mushrooms and spread in an unconsidered epidemic of sentimental concern for the 'oppressed' and 'downtrodden' and their unjustly poor *self-esteem*. *Self-esteem*, self-expression, assertiveness and self-centered lack of concern for rules seem to comprise the core curriculum of training in local government, industry and even the armed forces.

All this despite the fact that many social problems, including juvenile delinquency, crime, low work productivity and family collapse, are caused, not by low *self-esteem*, but by the excessively high *self-esteem* of many perpetrators.

A few programmes calculated to produce systematic reduction in self-esteem (we used to call it
humility) might be valuable.
DAVID MARSLAND

S EMINAR
Noun. An alternative form of academic
instruction less disciplined than the lecture; popular in new universities (qv); a gathering of pur-
portedly intelligent people who sit around pooling their ignorance until group findings emerge.
BRYAN WILSON

S HAME
Unknown to the post-modern lexicon, a word
discarded along with many other archaic words
such as decency, honesty, truth, Good and Evil (qv).
Shame lives only to be exploited by the mass
media. *Shame* dies with the crass and dissem-
bling behaviour of public figures. 'O *Shame*
where is thy blush?' (Hamlet).
GRAEME NEWMAN

S OCIAL
An adjective which automatically reverses the
meaning of any noun to which it is attached.
Thus a '*social* market economy' is not a market
economy, a '*social* worker' is not a worker, '*social*
democracy' is not democracy, '*social* theory' is
not theory, '*social* democrats' are not democrats
and '*social* justice' is not justice – indeed its pursuit involves and leads to injustice.
CHRISTIE DAVIES

S OVEREIGNTY, POOLED
An oxymoron, roughly equivalent to 'self-
government by others'. *Sovereignty* is the right,
power and freedom to make political decisions
without reference to any higher authority.
Strictly speaking it can inhere only in a single
individual or body, the 'sovereign', though the
sovereign may and does confer, by delegation,

many of its powers on subordinates and subjects. *Sovereignty* is not the (wholly imaginary) power to act uninfluenced or unconstrained by the co-existence of other, external, non-subject powers.

Pooled sovereignty is a euphemism devised by Euro-enthusiasts to describe, and disguise, the actual loss of national *sovereignty* consequent upon accepting the terms of the European Union. Though under those terms some rights of veto and exemption, which once acted to preserve a degree of national *sovereignty*, survive, they must surely be revoked before long, on account of the EU's continuing expansion. So far they have rarely been exercised and where they have not, *sovereignty* has forthwith been surrendered to the EU (for to surrender it here is inevitably, indeed by definition, to create it elsewhere).

So-called *pooled sovereignty* confers on each EU member a limited right, in concert with the others, to interfere in its fellow-members' previously 'internal' affairs. The price paid by each member for this right (a right which in any case none may particularly want or prize) is the parallel but much more extensive, indeed absolute, right of others, and of the EU as a whole, to interfere in that member's own internal affairs, and in a way that may be seriously contrary to its interest. So *pooled sovereignty* gives us all something that few want, the right to tell our neighbours how to live, in exchange for our permanently giving up (or throwing into the pool) something that all of us do want, or would want had we retained any self-respect, namely the right to decide for ourselves how we want to live.

What is at stake, of course, is the entire national idea. Once it, and the nation too, are swallowed up into the supranational state, the idea of a nation's 'internal affairs' or 'own business' vanishes along with them. What remains to be seen, and seems unlikely in the extreme, is

whether the popular allegiance previously vested in the nation, and inseparable from national *sovereignty*, can be transferred to the EU. If not, the EU must eventually either fall apart, or be held together not by consent, but by force. The only true supranational consent to be found in the EU at present seems to be that of its political and bureaucratic classes, a sentiment strongly reinforced by their common interests and (lavish) system of rewards and privileges.
ROBERT GRANT

S OVEREIGNTY, POOLING OF

A euphemism of handing over the powers currently exercised by nation-states to a supra-national bureaucracy such as the EU or various United Nations agencies. The main feature of such pooling is that national democratic deci-sion-making is substituted by that of supra-national administrative elites. It is the ENArques ' answer to Demos.
DEEPAK LAL

S PECULATION

Media-speak for a rumour in the future tense.
MARK SHIFFMAN

S TATE CAPITALISM

The name those opposed to capitalism (qv) give to non-capitalist economic systems they happen to disapprove of or are embarrassed by. It is a handy technique employed by today's anti-capitalists to disassociate themselves from the vast crimes committed in the name of anti-capi-talism in the twentieth century – and even asso-ciating supporters of capitalism with these crimes. It can also be used to argue that the abject failure of the non-capitalist system in the Soviet Union and Eastern Europe was not a fail-ure for the alternatives to capitalism, but a fail-ure of capitalism. A few anti-capitalists argue that the Soviet Union was *state-capitalist* from

its inception; others that it became *state-capitalist* with the rise of Joseph Stalin (ie when its murderous policies became too obvious to overlook); yet others only discovered that the Soviet Union was *state capitalist* after its the collapse.
MICHAEL MOSBACHER

S USTAINABLE
In need of subsidy from the taxpayer. As in 'To demonstrate that truly *sustainable* alternative (qv) energy will work requires governments have the courage (sic) to subsidize wave power'
MATT RIDLEY

S USTAINABLE as in SUSTAINABLE DEVELOPMENT
Sustainable development (qv)' is the watchword of innumerable brands of ecologists, environmentalists, New Age thinkers and devotees of 'Planet Earth'. They believe, no doubt rightly, that the degradation of the earth and the destruction of its peoples by unrestricted technological and industrial development can only be averted if such development can be kept within bounds.

They thus prefer a kind of modified Luddism, attractive to people who believe they can have their cake and eat it. Who will make them give up their cars? Who will decide what is *sustainable*? The limitation of industrial development they advocate could be enforced only by a world government which would have to control every aspect of human life. Would such a globale, totalitarian tyranny itself be *sustainable*?

Meanwhile the words *sustainable* and 'unsustainable' (qv) have acquired modish currency. They can now be applied vaguely to anything which affects the 'environment' (qv) or the 'community' (qv), usually adversely as in a recent official pronouncement: 'the building of executive homes for commuters in the countryside is unacceptable and unsustainable', when in fact it

is perfectly *sustainable* until the money runs out.
MICHAEL WHARTON

TAINTED
Used to mean contaminated. Now used metaphorically with one particular application. This is to dismiss someone else's views on the grounds that they have received funds from incorrect sources. The notion of 'taint' saves the denouncer a great deal of work. He does not have to show any argument against the views with which he disagrees. It is a version of demonisation by association. Interestingly the demonic character of the 'tainting' body does not have to be established by argument either. Top league 'tainters' are predictably the CIA, multinational corporations and rich right-wing (qv) men. No 'taint' is taken by a person receiving funding from an NGO, international organization or a government department seeking legitimation for increased regulation or spending.
MICHAEL MOSBACHER

THIRD as in the THIRD WAY
A new phrase for an old error. The doctrine and practice of a middle route between the market and socialism. It holds that there is a form of social market capitalism, or social democracy, or free enterprise modified by communitarianism, which avoids both the greed and atomism of the capitalist economy and the inefficiency and brutal coercion of full socialism. The doctrine has much in common with the Catholic economic tradition of the last 130 years (which Catholics are not, however, obliged to accept) which condemns all-out capitalism as materialistic. The European corporatist approach to capitalism, which informs the practice of all the powers in the EU except Britain, is related to this Catholic tradition and therefore to the *Third Way*. Its major political exponent in Britain today is Tony Blair. Its major academic light is

Anthony Giddens. Paradoxically, despite the popularity of the Labour Government since 1997, they have not persuaded many people in Britain of the cogency of the *Third Way*, which sounds, as Eamonn Butler has put it, as if it might lead to the Third World.

The doctrine is fatally flawed. Capitalism is a never fully-realized ideal type. All market economies have large sectors not regulated by market principles. The debate concerns the degree of pre-eminence given to the market. International comparison shows that for economic dynamism, the Anglo-American model of relatively untrammelled markets is most effective, vis B vis living standards, full employment and technological innovation. The *Third Way* relies heavily on state activity. It will inevitably perform badly against economies with less state involvement. With the eclipse of Keynesianism, the *Third Way* has no theory and thus compares unfavourably with neo-libertarianism. The *Third Way* joins social democracy and corporatism as atheoretical doctrines stranded between a true theory, or at least a free-market theory broadly vindicated by the evidence, and the false theories of socialism, tested out and vitiated during the course of the twentieth century. It is really a doctrine for those who know nothing about economics.

DENNIS O'KEEFFE

TRANSPARENCY

It was once a physical quality, that of transmitting rays of light without diffusion so that bodies behind can easily be seen (Concise Oxford Dictionary). During the 1960s, however, there arose a fashion for educational technology, a prominent part of which was devoted to the worship of 'visual aids'. The defining article in the cult was the *transparency*. Having and being able to show one's *transparencies* in sequence and the right way up or being able to intone 'next *transparency* please' with the right note of nonchalance was all part of that other sixties cult, the weekend 'residential' in a country house run by a 'bursar'-housekeeper couple on the fiddle. The house was cold and the food bad – because of the fiddling. Along with the *transparencies* went name tags, large felt tip pens, lists of targets, flow charts, psychological games in which participants revealed themselves and a certain amount of adultery.

Now that the 'business community' had appropriated the word it found exciting new uses for it. And it has recently re-surfaced in a new cult, that of accountability and openness. Once managers and others were responsible for their results. Increasingly not only their results must be seen but also the minutiae of their procedures. Indeed, so intense is the scrutiny of procedures that results are often forgotten. The contemporary modern (qv) bureaucracy, be it in the public (qv) or private sector, and notably including schools and the NHS, consists of a large body of staff devising correct procedures for an even larger body of staff to follow obsessively and counter-productively with yet another group evaluating the first two and an expensive outside body checking that the procedures fit wider norms of quality (qv) control. If there is one tendency in politics, business and the professions that could successfully destroy all of them, it is the once innocent *transparency*.
DIGBY ANDERSON

U NDERPRIVILEGED

Euphemistic weasel word used by ideologues who do not like to say 'poor'. Its usage is absurd. What does it mean to be *underprivileged*? It can be contrasted only with 'overprivileged'. Does the speaker wish to maintain that there is an ideal state which is neither 'under' nor 'over' but merely 'privileged'? But where everyone is privileged, no-one is privileged. Besides, the use of this euphemism fails in its intention to arouse sympathy. I am truly sorry for Tom who is genuinely poor, and so I might be encouraged to help him. But when I hear that Dick is only *underprivileged*, I can pass by on the other side without trouble to my conscience.

The same goes for 'partially-sighted' (blind); 'hearing-impaired' (deaf). And what violence these euphemisms do to the language! What, are we to say 'as partially-sighted as a bat' or 'as hearing-impaired as a post'!

PETER MULLEN

U NEMPLOYMENT

Strictly defined, the situation of someone who does not have a job and is actively searching for one. However, many 'unemployed' have been so for a long time and cannot truthfully be said to be 'active in their search'. The reason is that their situation has been complicated by the availability of state payments of 'benefits' (qv) both for remaining unemployed and for taking a low-paid job. Furthermore, in many economies strong unions or other barriers such as a minimum wage actually prevent them from offering their labour freely at a wage of their choice. These things worsen the well-known problem that when the economy goes through a slump, it becomes harder to find a job; for the efforts of unconstrained people looking for one would help to get them back to work over time.

Unfortunately, the word is often used with the connotation that those unemployed can have no power over their situation and that the state has a duty to eradicate *unemployment* by stimulating the economy. What we now know is that if the state does any such thing, it will, after a short interval, only produce inflation; but that the state can indeed reduce *unemployment* by first removing the minimum wage laws and the powers of trade unions that prevent people from

freely offering their labour, and secondly removing the entitlement to endless *unemployment* benefit that discourages people from offering to work at a wage employers can afford to pay. All this is sadly the opposite of what participants in the BBC's Question Time usually have in mind.
PATRICK MINFORD

U NIT

When the Social Affairs Unit was established in 1980, the term was chosen as signifying a group and conveying rather more modest hopes than an 'institute'. Since then it has acquired pejorative associations as a result of Government attempts to reduce the pleasures of the social drinking of good wine to the mere consumption of *units* of alcohol.
DIGBY ANDERSON

U NIVERSITY

1. (Archaic) A body of masters and students devoted to a common study of the liberal arts, philosophy and theology, in pursuit of universal knowledge and 'true enlargement of mind which is the power of viewing many things at once as one whole' (John Henry, Cardinal Newman). 2. In current usage, an institution host to a number of scholars engaged in attaining and maintaining standing in their respective fields of study by producing journal articles, conference papers, books and making television appearances. Students at a *university* are provided with opportunities (qv) to gain preliminary acquaintance with these various fields or to serve as audience to preliminary rehearsals or recapitulations of these various products.

Professors lead students in a study of the construction and deconstruction of 'worlds of discourse'. Since the unifying principle of this endeavour is the raw potential of the students to pursue any of the studies available, the further the progress of their education the less unified the whole becomes. Hence the increasingly common locution '*university* community (qv)', which, insofar as it is felt to be necessary, testifies to its own falsehood. At its highest level of achievement, a *university* provides an institutional home for specialized experts incapable of communicating with one another. In thus eroding the possibilities for tolerant conversation about shared undertakings, which is the grounding of civil (qv) community and genuine education, the *university* becomes a struggle of all against all, so that its only recourse is to cede all sovereignty over itself to the Bureaucratic Leviathan whose name is Administration.

MARK SHIFFMAN

U NSUSTAINABLE

This word no longer means that the practice to which it refers cannot continue. Instead it means that the speaker does not like the practice and hopes it will soon come to an end. '*Unsustainable* development (qv)' is development of which the speaker does not approve. '*Capitalism* (qv) is *unsustainable*' means that the speaker is anti-capitalist – it has taken the place of 'capitalism will collapse under the weight of its own contradictions'. 'The welfare state is *unsustainable*' or 'the Euro is *unsustainable*' means that the speaker does not approve of the welfare state or the Euro. When something is described as *unsustainable* it is now an opinion of worth and not a prophecy.

MICHAEL MOSBACHER

V ALID

A useful word for suppressing other people's ethical and aesthetic judgements. To say Mick Hucknall of Simply Red is as good as Mozart, though striking a blow against outdated music, is to perpetuate elitist notions of 'good'. Mr Hucknall is therefore as valid as Mozart, and rather more so in 'arts' programmes like Radio 4's

Front Row, most music courses at new universities (qv), etc.

JOHN MALONEY

VICTIM

One who, through no fault of his or her own, can be held responsible for nothing. Prominent victims are teenage delinquents, criminals (qv), illegal immigrants, single parents, many public sector workers, many trades unionists, the unemployed, homosexuals and child molestors. They are all *victims* of our uncaring society and, as a result, none is in any way to blame for his or her actions.

SIMON HEFFER

VIOLENCE

A word of abuse applied by ideologues to anything they don't like. Thus we receive the perverted expressions: the *violence* of poverty (qv); the *violence* of capitalism (qv); the *violence* of silence; the *violence* of language; the *violence* of inequality (qv); the *violence* of global warming. The meaning of this word would be lost forever if it were not for the popular and innovative movie Bonnie and Clyde (1967) starring Warren Beatty, which established graphic *violence* as a medium all its own. The replication of such bloody scenes over and over again in hundreds of movies since that time ensured that true *violence* would find its proper place in the hearts and minds of the masses.

GRAEME NEWMAN

VISION

(Functional synonym: Realism, often enough 'gritty') (Indicative antonyms: Clarity, Modesty) The *Vision* without which, we are so often told by the Glibocracy, 'the people perish' was, in the minds of the prophets, a spontaneous irruption into human consciousness of the Divine will. It came, that is, from a higher place and was neither generated by human capacity or ambition nor designed for human purpose or aggrandisement. Indeed, Revelation 22 v18 promises punishment to any human being who meddles in *Vision*. It is, of course, common these days for what were once exclusively God-like attributes to be shared out amongst, or annexed by human beings. Oddly, for a secular age, when so transposed, such attributes retain in the secular world some of their original potency, although in making the transition they move from sanctity to sanctimoniousness.

Politicians are prone to lay claim to *vision*. President Bush's magnificent diffidence about 'the *Vision* thing' marks him out as a very sensible man and an unusual politician. President Clinton and Mr Blair are *vision*-politicians. Their *vision* is, of course, entirely self-conferred: and by it they mean that all who disagree with them are not merely disagreeable but terminally purblind and damned. Radical clerics, foxed by the rather obvious conservatism of their congregations, promulgate an episcopal *vision* which pours the persuasive blindness of light on an endless series of technical subjects on which such clerics are knowledgeable only when self-blinded by *vision*. Promiscuous (qv) *vision* of this clerical kind feeds on itself: so that, for example, a cleric concerned to legitimize homosexual unions in the Church of England could refer to a Lambeth Conference rejection of such things as equivalent to a 'Nuremberg Rally'. Vision, self-induced, of human derivation, overwhelms both tradition and reason. It is ignorance triumphant.
JON DAVIES

V OCATIONAL
Strictly speaking a calling, as in the priesthood or in medicine. Now used to refer to any type of course or training whose only value is instrumental, the less sacred, the more *vocational*. A term much used by those who

would deprive our system of education of any aspiration (qv) to excellence (qv) and for whom the very idea of a calling or a priesthood is an anachronism.

ANTHONY O'HEAR

WAY as in THE THIRD WAY

Much has been said about *the third way*; most of it asking whether it is really a new politics as the term third (qv) is taken to imply. But what of *way*? *Way* is part of the traditional language of political ideology. It belongs with road, highway and signpost as the language of the political journey or pilgrimage. The other leading political analogy is that of construction, building the new society, the reconstruction of Europe, bricks and mortar.

So there is nothing new in using the term *way* in politics. However, *way* made some sense as an image in the old (qv) politics because the old politics was about policies to make a difference, to lead a people to somewhere different, a new promised land. But what many commentators have noticed about *the third way* is that it is a politics of pose, spin and gesture, a curiously non-ideological politics, a politics going nowhere. This may be good news. Unspeakable miseries have been caused by some of the great marches and journeys that utopian politicians have led their people on. But is is surely odd that a new politics proclaiming the word *way* should be new chiefly in the sense that it goes nowhere. It might be better termed dead-end politics.

DIGBY ANDERSON

WELFARE

Properly means a person's well-being. However, because of the state's overwhelming intrusion into 'social (qv) affairs', it has come to mean the state's provision of benefits (qv), even though these reduce the *welfare* of not merely taxpayers but also recipients (in the long term).

Thus we have the 'welfare state', being 'on the welfare', 'cutting off welfare benefits' as popular terms – eg Eastenders, passim. Most recently, New Labour has come to suggest 'welfare reform'; this is a hopeful development, like getting a poacher to turn gamekeeper. Apparently, Messrs Blair and Brown have become convinced that the way to cut state spending on benefits and improve employment is to – surprise, surprise – be tough on providing benefits to those who do not work; when back in work these people will claim less benefit than out of it. Since it was originally Labour that pushed up these benefit entitlements for their own constituency as they saw it, New Labour has the best chance of reducing them. The Tories delivered the middle classes over market reform; will New Labour deliver the 'working classes' over welfare reform?

PATRICK MINFORD

WORK WITH

To fatally undermine another's work, project or ambitions. A politician who announces he is 'working with' a colleague means he is either just about to sack him – or he is about to be sacked himself. The statement 'I am happy to work with Mr X in my cabinet' means 'either he goes or I go, but he is the one who will be going'.

'Work' used to be one of the most respectable words in the English dictionary, but it has spent the past decade slumming it in the world of psychobabble. Seduced from its original meaning of Newtonian work – the energy required to move a physical object from one place to another – it now means the energy required to dredge up emotions; diffuse, unfocused, hysterical and exhausting. To work with somebody is to work upon his emotions, to force him to make irrational decisions based on his feelings rather than the facts. This makes him feel inadequate, helpless and unable to proceed.

It is also a form of female bullying much

favoured in the new gynocratic offices. The same technique is used by mothers when they bend down to correct the behaviour of a naughty toddler. 'Look at me directly Toby when I am talking to you.' The very act of being forced to look at your questioner brings on a feeling of guilt. In modern management, mothers' questions are replaced with 'personal development plans'. These are humiliating diaries in which victims are forced to keep a daily record of their failings and intentions to reform. Personal development plans create a sense of self loathing so severe that very few can bear to open them after a few weeks. They can then be sacked.

By 'working with' male colleagues, ambitious young women can rise very rapidly in an organization. It allows them to take over projects, poach ideas and eliminate threatening innovations. The difficulty arises when, having cleared the office of males, they try to *work with* each other. *Work with* is also replacing that threadbare euphemism, 'helping the police with their enquiries'.

If somebody offers to *work with* you, flee.
MYLES HARRIS

X ENOPHOBE

Formerly meant someone who suffered a fear of foreigners. It is now used exclusively by advocates of a United States of Europe to describe in one word anyone in Britain who questions any aspect of the European Union, in particular the Common Fisheries Policy, the Common Agricultural Policy, any fraud or other misdemeanour of a Commissioner, or any of the Regulations and Directives they propose. For example: 'The Cornish fishermen, *xenophobes* to a man, are once again complaining that the Spaniards are taking all their fish'.

The word can also be used as a succinct answer to any argument about the European Union. In the privacy of their own home, Euro enthusiasts use this word repetitively and with mounting anger to themselves in order to relieve their feelings.

RICHARD BODY

X ENOPHOBIA

Still means a marked dislike of foreigners. It has changed however in two respects. First it is now deeply disapproved of. Secondly, a dislike of foreigners is not now considered odd or disapproved of by intellectuals if the foreigner is American.

Should 250 million Americans not afford sufficient object for the hatred of intellectuals, then it is permissible for English intellectuals to hate their own country and tradition as well. This privilege is not extended to French intellectuals who must still revere France and her traditions. They are allowed, in compensation, double rations of anti-Americanism.

DIGBY ANDERSON

Y OUTH

Youth has always, until now, had as one connotation that of inexperience, ignorance and ineptitude. Correspondingly, old age is associated with wisdom and judgement. Modern society increasingly tends to deify youth. This has bizarre consequences in politics and even more distressing effects on adults who now feel obliged to dress, speak and behave like young people.

DIGBY ANDERSON

Z IONIST

Before 1948 someone who believed that Jews could only escape anti-Semitic racism through the establishment of a Jewish state – an argument first popularized in modern times by Theodor Herzl in 1896 in his Der Judenstaat, or 'The State of the Jews'. This argument was widely felt to have been borne out by the horrors visited upon Jewry by Nazi Germany.

After 1948 a *Zionist* was someone who supported the state of Israel. Progressive opinion was fairly sympathetic to 'Zionism' and then Israel in the aftermath of the war, partly as a response to the holocaust and partly because the *Zionist* movement had a strong, although by no means exclusive, socialist component. Progressive opinion of Zionism soon changed rapidly. Perhaps this change was spearheaded by the Soviet Union, which soon started to describe internal opponents as *Zionists*. In this context *Zionist* had no meaning, other than as to smear that person. It was one of a panoply of abuses the Soviet Union used against opponents – others included anti-Soviet, revanchist, imperialist, and Trotskyite. These too had no meaning. They were terms of execration. It soon also became de rigour among progressive opinion in the west to use *Zionist* as a term of abuse. The most bizarre trend was to equate Zionism – a movement whose raison d'être was a response to and salvation from racism – with racism. This pejorative use of the word Zionism still lives on amongst those who have perhaps not quite noticed that the Soviet Union, and the panoply of abuse it used, has come to an end. The progressive use of *Zionist* as a term of abuse has enabled post-war Nazis and anti-Semites to hide behind the term when peddling their old hatred.

MICHAEL MOSBACHER

BY DIGBY ANDERSON

To celebrate the Social Affairs Unit's twentieth birthday, we asked authors who have written for us and friends who have shown an interest in our work over those years to contribute to this dictionary. They chose the words. We simply specified the words should be words which once meant something good and now mean something bad, which once meant something and now mean nothing or vice versa, or which have in some interesting sense changed.

It is a dictionary of dangerous words. The writers of prefaces to dictionaries are forever pointing out that language is a living thing and constantly changes. The meaning of words changes. But it seldom does so totally and for everyone. The words in this dictionary are dangerous for precisely this reason. They have acquired new uses and meanings for some people in some situations. Their new associations are rarely declared outright.

Thus, the dictionary starts with access. It used to mean a way into a building or service such as a school or healthcare. Once you had or did not have access. Now everyone ought to have access and when they do not this is an injustice which ought to be rectified. They have, everyone has a right to access and if they do not find their way into a university or if they don't use the state-subsidized theatre because they find Shakespeare boring, then their right of access has been denied.

This new meaning of access depends on a whole baggage of opinions about rights, whether everyone has them and whether all the institutions in question are rightfully everyone's, about justice and about injustice, about the obligations that go with subsidy and with attending the theatre. Sometimes these ideas are declared and argued for explicitly. More often, the repeated use of the word in the new sense just acquires it the connotation of a good thing.

A large proportion of the words in the dictionary

carry this ideological baggage. What ideology is it? Egalitarianism and extended rights are a frequent theme of the entries. So a word only a few entries from access, affirm, is increasingly used in educational circles to describe a need and a right which all children are said to have, to be affirmed. Not only do all children need to be affirmed, whether they do well or badly at school, but some imply that they need equal amounts of affirmation. Yet another instance of rights-thinking is the entry for aspiration. The modern tendency is to describe increasing numbers of the good things of this world as aspirations with the new connotation that aspirations ought to be satisfied.

The satisfaction of equal rights and aspirations is a fairly tall order and those who espouse them are likely to find themselves also taking up an oppositionalist stance, to try to correct and tidy the world. Thus the new use of alternative does not just describe another way of doing things but a better way. Tidying the world means taking control of it; in this ideology there is no putting up with reality or learning to live with pain and grief, so accident has changed; accidents don't happen by accident any longer. There is always a culprit to be found who has inflicted them on the victim and a new preventive procedure to install to prevent them happening again.

Making sure the world is as it ought to be means correcting language as in the new use of appropriate to indicate which words may be used to refer to, for instance, Gypsies, the mentally ill or homosexuals. It involves the quaint notion that changing language will alter the things words describe so the campaign is on to manipulate the names given to, eg disabled persons and black people in the hope this will change the unkind treatment of the people themselves. Words such as quality assurance and code of practice make similar assumptions, in their case that by monitoring procedures in a bureaucratic way, outcomes will be improved. Thus codes of practice and quality assurance are good things.

The solutions involved in putting the world to rights are often highly collective so compassion is increasingly used of state actions as well as those of individuals and national problems can be made international matters by wider and wider use of the word, genocide and the tortured metaphor, the pooling of sovereignty. One of the easiest ways to tidy the world is to have a thorough linguistic clear-out so several words once widely used are just thrown out or kept solely to mock when the day gets dull. They include honour, fortitude, patriotism, manliness, gentleman, marriage and perversion. To compensate, some other words which once had a restricted use are littered throughout conversation; the most mentioned ubiquitous newcomer is partner. Yet others have lost all meaning except disapproval. Unsustainable does not mean cannot be sustained but should not be sustained. Violence, as in the violence of capitalism or the violence of poverty just means I disapprove.

By no means all words fit into these categories. The bizarre use of amazing by journalists to describe an event when they have no notion whether it will indeed amaze anyone, or the same journalists' description of the price of CDs as frightening is just that, bizarre.

But there is no doubt that the new use of the majority of words in the dictionary is ideological. And there is no doubt that the ideology in question is liberalism – in the American sense of that word, socialistic-progressive. There is not one word which has changed its meaning towards a conservative or reactionary ideal. In economics, capitalism may be the only show in town. But in culture – if words do indicate culture – there is no question. It is firmly in the grip of the liberals. I am not sure theirs is not the greater victory.

The sheer number of words which have been ideologically appropriated goes far beyond this little dictionary. It poses a tricky question for writers and speakers who do not share the ideology concerned. How do they write or speak without endorsing the ideology?

THE AUTHORS

Dr LINCOLN ALLISON is Reader in Politics, University of Warwick.

Dr DIGBY ANDERSON is founder Director of the Social Affairs Unit.

JOHN BLUNDELL is General Director of the Institute of Economic Affairs.

Sir RICHARD BODY MP is Member of Parliament for Boston and Skegness.

TODD BREYFOGLE is a Fellow of Liberty Fund Inc, Indianapolis.

Dr EAMONN BUTLER is Director of the Adam Smith Institute.

Professor CHRISTIE DAVIES is Professor of Sociology, University of Reading.

Dr THEODORE DALRYMPLE is an inner city and prison GP and writes for The Spectator.

Dr JON DAVIES teaches in the Department of Religious Studies, University of Newcastle-upon-Tyne.

Professor ANTONY FLEW is Professor Emeritus of Philosophy, University of Reading.

FREDERICK FORSYTH is a best-selling author; his books include The Day of the Jackal.

Dr CHARLES GOODSON-WICKES is a barrister and physician.

Professor JULIUS GOULD is Chairman of the Trustees of the Social Affairs Unit.

Dr ROBERT GRANT is Reader in English, University of Glasgow.

Dr SIMON GREEN is a Fellow of All Souls' College, Oxford.

JOHN GREENWOOD is a businessman and Treasurer of the Social Affairs Unit.

Lord HARRIS OF HIGH CROSS is President of the Institute of Economic Affairs.

Dr MYLES HARRIS is a general practitioner and journalist.

SIMON HEFFER writes for the Daily Mail, New Statesman, and is the biographer of Enoch Powell.

DERRICK HILL writes for the Daily Mail.

PETER HITCHENS writes for The Express and is the author of The Abolition of Britain.